THE

ELEMENTS

OF

DESIGN

By a Quintessential Designer

Written by Don Hadfield through a period
from 1985 to 2017

This book is dedicated to:

Norm McNernery, my mentor, whose wisdom and guidance shaped my career as a young engineer and consider him, the best engineer I ever worked with.

Karen, my wife, Matt and Andrea, my children, who have endured my engineer traits. I am a better engineer because, Karen allowed me to concentrate on engineering, while, among many other things, took care of everything on the home front.

Table of Contents

Introduction

A Master designing a device, in tune with The Elements of Design+: using the Design Process while in the Zone, dancing with the Creative Spirit, abiding by nature's physical and spiritual laws, questioning all the answers in a humble way, yielding to a higher logic, iterating to simplicity, and striving for perfection but settling for excellence while living a balanced life—this is what the book covers in a nutshell

The book is short; the fewer the words, the more powerful they are.

In outline form, with each page having the chapter name at the top and the page number on the bottom, allows quick reference to any part of the book. The form is similar to Elements of Style by Strunk and White.

Many of the thoughts and analogies can be used in any type of engineering or in other disciplines. Ponder the thoughts and apply them in a discerning manner.

In this book, there are no new concepts or revelations; it is based on common sense, scientific facts, and thoughts throughout the ages. Even though there are many powerful tools and technologies, computer-aided design (CAD) software being a major one, the Elements of Design+ remain timeless. The compilation of the subjects (elements) is what makes the book unique. Most of the thoughts were derived in the context of creating equipment for in-plant use to build the company's products.

This book is not intended to be all encompassing; that's why it's called Elements of Design+. The elements covered played a major role in Mr. Hadfield's machine design career. Included [that's why there is a + in the title] are quotes, philosophies and

Introduction

humor that one might find interesting. They were pondered and lived, thereby, building and molding the complex soul of a machine designer. The humor is a glimpse of the author's favorites, and was added for some light heartiness.

He believes that for best results, one must have a passion for what they are doing. They must be focused and have concentrated efforts while in the Zone.

Who should read this book? Young engineers, engineering managers, as well as experienced engineers. This book would be very helpful for an engineer just starting out, as it explains many aspects of engineering. Managers, especially those who don't have a design background, would find this book useful in learning what they are dealing with. Experienced engineers can read and enjoy it, saying to themselves, "Yeah, that's the way it is or should be!" They may even show it to their boss for various reasons left unsaid here!

There are many nuggets that stand by themselves and can be used to make a point or to teach.

Enjoy the book!

About the Author

Don Hadfield was born an engineer. As a child in Southeastern Massachusetts, he built everything from go-karts to tree houses (one spanning four trees). With age, came more complex projects, including building a Van der Graaf generator, experimental electric motors, and a modular, full sized, office desk that fit in his compact car. As a student, math, science, and mechanical drawing escalated his hobbies to an academic track and led him to focus his studies in machine design at the University of Massachusetts Lowell. He graduated with a Bachelor of Science in Mechanical Engineering.

With a career spanning over four decades, Don's major jobs were at Simplex Wire & Cable (13 years), Gould (10 years), and Hewlett Packard/Phillips (19 years). Each company allowed Don to hone his skills from engineering of tools and equipment to state-of-the-art, next- generation product design and fabrication processes that are still used in the healthcare industry today. In his roles, he valued the importance of understanding the vision of his leaders and translating it with extreme precision in every project he led.

Elements of Design+ by a Quintessential Designer is Don's third publication. In 1987, he wrote a guide entitled Machine Design and Related Subjects, which focused on the basic truths of in-plant machine design and described the fundamental mantras of the machine design process. In 1990, he wrote a book called Truths to Live By, a guide to successful living.

A lifetime learner, Don maintains relationships with his mentors and mentees in the field. They are the finest reflection of his career. Now technically retired, Don spends most of his time between the Seacoast Region of New Hampshire and the South Coast of Massachusetts with his wife, Karen. Often joined by their son of Newport, Rhode Island and daughter of

About the Author

Boston, Massachusetts as well as their families, Don can be found describing complex systems of everyday life—once an engineer, always an engineer.

Design Process

Design Process

Machine design is an art, a science, a trade, and a profession. The big part of the process is working with the laws of nature. Nature's laws are unwavering, which is a solace to the designer. Designing a device is like a test given in the laws of nature. Violate them and you fail. Violate the spiritual laws and you will also fail. Being in tune with all the natural laws, laws of physics, etc. is a great help in visualizing the concepts, allowing one to dance more effectively with the creative spirit while in the zone. Also, being in tune with people of all disciplines is a big part of machine design. Machine design is analogous to a servo guidance system. At the beginning, a designer is given input (information), which sets him/her on a course to design a device [could be a system, machine or component)]. As the task proceeds, one must dig for information from within the workplace, from fabrication people or those using it; perform analysis in the form of basic research and various calculations. All these learnings become new input (information and knowledge) to guide one through the design. This input usually forces many corrections in the course. In fact, they may contradict the inputs given at the beginning. In the end, more often than not, the design is quite different than original concepts i.e., the course changed many times during the design

1 Initial Design Cycle/Questioning Can I do this job?

   Is it over my head? Can I get In the zone? Will I have the drive? Bewilderment

   Is there a better way?

   Do I have all that is needed? Can it be reverse engineered?

   Can it be bought instead of designing it?

Design Process

2   Design Approach

Step #1: Formulate the ideal solution forgetting whether it's possible or not

Step #2: Identify the barriers that lie between you and your shining goal. You have to be fearless and cannot be stopped by anything

Step #3: Is when you ask, what is the heart of the problem? Once you have that, all else is a chain of technicalities. A related question is, under what conditions does the problem cease to exist? This step is very time consuming, so there is always a big temptation to cut corners, but you pay in the end. [Steven Ashley, August 1986, Popular Science, p 84]

3   Focused effort is mandatory [see The Zone chapter, Item 1, 10]

4   Intuitive visualizations form by dancing with the creative spirit

5   Information gathering

6   Creativity, cascading being an integral part, and unconventional thinking is crucial to the design process [See Creativity chapter]

7   Passion for excellence

8   Mind inertia

Design Process

Happens with a concentrated effort for long continuous periods of time. [see The Zone Chapter, Item 10]

9   Reality checks

10 Continual questioning of direction, assumptions and design

11 Evolution

12 Simplification

13 Consolidating

14 Experimentation

15 Experience

16 Look to nature for ideas

All nature is using the same building blocks, elements, molecules, etc.

It has taken nature billions of years to create its magnificent creatures, structures and landscapes. Why not take advantage of it and leverage off it, just like Leonardo Da Vinci did.

LEONARDO DA VINCI (1452-1519) THE GREATEST GENIUS THE WORL.D HAS EVER KNOWN?

Leonardo da Vinci has been widely celebrated as a leading Renaissance painter and sculptor, but he was also known as an engineer and scientist .... It is only relatively

Design Process

recently that analysis of his full body of work has led us to realize the true scope of his genius he truly was one of the greatest inventors, artists, scientists and thinkers of all time .... From Leonardo's quest to learn everything there was to know .... he learned through the power of observation and experience a skill he would apply to everything he did, for the rest of his life. A tireless observer, Leonardo was fascinated by the study of nature. He was a great student of light and shadow riveted by the effects created by multiple light sources upon faces and objects. This deep curiosity with nature found expression in every sort of artistic discipline. He was unique among his contemporaries in using his scientific observations to enrich his paintings and sculptures, which often demonstrated extraordinary precision and accuracy.

Leonardo was also a military strategist inventing the tank, the bullet and bridges of amazing ingenuity. In fact, Leonardo made remarkable contributions to every field which he applied himself, from geology to astronomy, anatomy to cartography. He dreamed of creating the "ideal city" with a healthy environment that would rid the world of the plague. He foreshadowed the invention of the automobile, improved ball bearing, gearing systems and sketched the mechanisms for a robot. But at the basic level, it all came back to that deep captivation with nature. All Leonardo's inventions are founded in nature's principles. "Though human ingenuity may make various inventions .... it will never devise any inventions more beautiful, nor more simple, nor more to the purpose than nature does; because, in her inventions nothing is wanting, and nothing is superfluous." – Leonardo da Vinci

PHYSICS AND MECHANICAL PRINCIPLES

Design Process

"I have been impressed with the urgency of doing. Knowing is not enough we must apply. Be willing is not enough: we must do." – Leonardo da Vinci. Leonardo believed that mechanics was the key understanding the world. He studied interactions of water, air and light and identified patterns in their behavior under different circumstances. He depicted swirling water, moving air currents, and shadows and reflections of light in drawings as he strove to understand the underlying physical and mechanical principles.

To Leonardo, the human body was a complex and advanced machine capable of a wide range of movements. He explored the questions of how anatomy shapes physical behavior in animals and humans, and how humans express their feelings. Above all he wondered: what are the hidden mechanisms that govern life itself?

Leonardo believed that if he could reach an understanding of the workings of human action and natural forces, he could create machines that replicated the patterns of nature. His studies on mechanics, anatomy and physiognomy (the art of determining character traits based on the appearance of the face or body) underpinned most of his activities and inventions. Some of Leonardo's mechanical achievements include flywheels, ball bearing coil systems, coil springs, transformation of motion and the eccentric cam.

[Da Vinci, THE GENIUS, Exhibit Museum of Science, Boston December 14, 2016]

17 Optimum design's destruction

Design Process

17.1 Lack of time

17.2 Quality time is a must to develop optimum designs which contain 'absolutes' and 'building blocks' for future designs. [see Building Blocks chapter]

17.3 Specific design directives/ideas demanded

18 Un-groove your thinking

To find a simpler, better or more optimum design.

19 Learn the driving force phrases that help evolve it to the optimum design.

Too complicated-simplify it

Too expensive

Ugly

Hard to assemble

Hard to fabricate

New information

New features needed

Brainstorming

Seek other opinions

Design Process

20 Diversity

Diversity of design to accomplish the same thing. Many times, there are 100$^+$ different designs that might be done. 50 will work, the other 50 are either very poor or will not work. Within the 50 that work, two or three are excellent designs and maybe one will be astounding: simply elegant.

21 Suggestions and Directives

In starting the job, suggestions will be given by the lead designers, managers, marketing people or customers [the people who will buy or use it].

Never take anything for granted. Never say, I did what you wanted and it didn't work. It's up to the designer to question all the answers. When there are discrepancies they should be talked about, so everyone understands the track taken. The details will drive it. In the end, the designer will know how it works and how to use it better than anyone.

Throughout the process of designing and building a device, suggestions, inferences and ideas will be given. If the designer feels he could design and build the device using different concepts that would be faster and more reliable than suggested methods at a reasonable cost, then he should do so. However, it is the responsibility of the designer to build the device in a timely manner within the budget that functions to the customer's satisfaction. If the job is done properly, there will be many tweaks related to feedback from people that might use or make it. Along the way, there may be quantum jumps in either

Design Process

direction, forward or backward. Question all the answers all the time, no matter who they come from. When ideas or information are given, consider the source; verify to your satisfaction that the information is correct

Always give credit to whomever comes up with the ideas.

22 Learn to work with all types.

People can be deceiving, change their minds, have bad hair days, have hidden agendas, forgetful, inaccurate, reprogram themselves and are variable unlike the laws of nature.

23 One must be in touch with reality and in tune with nature's laws

24 Always be willing to yield to a higher logic [see The Master chapter, Item 33]

The designer must keep communicating with all levels of people that may have input or are impacted by the design in any way, remembering to question all the answers and to yield to the higher logic.

Minimize the ego and use the best ideas no matter where they come from: the factory floor, peers, customers or even the president. The designer cannot foresee or know everything, so he must observe, listen and ask questions. The factory floor personnel have experience. They are extra eyes and ears for the designer. Remember: give credit to those who come up with ideas that you use.

Design Process

Engineers have a logic, why they might want to do something a certain way, but there might be a simpler way to do the same thing. One must always be receptive to simplification.

Minimizing the ego allows one to be more in tune with his surroundings and much more perceptive. Be aware of the environment it's going into. Design it to survive in that environment. Design it to take abuse.

As the truths become known, one becomes very strong and unyielding, usually making convincing arguments for doing it the right way.

If it's 'six of one and half a dozen of another', do it the way the person doing it or using it prefers. That develops ownership and the person's worth and acceptance

25 It is never right for a designer to say, "I did what you wanted and it doesn't work"

26 Ask questions

One should never be embarrassed to ask questions; one can't know everything. Go to the experts for the answers whenever possible. One can find the answers from many resources.

27 After it is out in the field being used

The people using it will know how it works and how to use it better than anyone. This is the best time for the designer to go out and talk to them. What do or don't they like about the design?This is excellent feedback for the

Design Process

designer. Now is the time to reflect on the project and ask, "If I was doing the job again, what would I do the same way or what would I do different?"

28 One must sell his ideas

It's an easier sell, if the idea came from the customer

29 Designing within the window

In designing a device there are important parameters that have a range of values.

Example: Design a module that inserts a cork into a wine bottle.

This module could be part of an automatic bottling machine or a standalone device.

Find the force limits of inserting the cork into the bottle, by running tests on natural and synthetic corks. Let's say, the loads varied from 40 to 60 pounds. It's impossible to test all variations of natural and synthetic corks. One needs to increase the high value and decrease the lower one. So, for the design use a range of 30 to 70.

The module must work perfectly, through the whole range of 30 to 70 pounds [the window].

30 Design Reviews

Design reviews are okay for general information, spotting major problems or scheduling. Meetings should include people with a broad knowledge of the company's

Design Process

platforms, that the design might interface with. Meetings are not for details. They are best with the designer and others, who mutually respect one another, conducted at the designer's desk or small room.

Have a design review on a very limited number of very important details.

Brainstorming can be an important tool in design

The goal must be clear so that brains are focused on the problems to be solved.

Sessions can be helpful if done with the right mixture of people, such as customers, peers, superiors, marketing personnel, research and development people, maintenance staff, machinists, mechanics or millwrights, to name a few, who all have a different set of experiences and thoughts in their heads that can be tapped into. Multiple minds are better than one at various stages of the design process. Don't be afraid to say something stupid. This can lead to becoming un- grooved, (i.e., thinking in a different way or thinking out of the box).

Don't allow a committee to call all the shots.

Designed by committee is not a compliment. The designs can be reviewed by committee. A committee may come up with some ideas that should be incorporated in the design. At the beginning of the project, there must be a strong individual or champion that has the vision and will to drive the design to its simplest and most effective form in a timely manner

Design Process

31 Engineer the machine to work the first time

Building it will test the correctness of the theories and calculations. When necessary, do quick experiments to check out a theory that you are basing the design on. Whenever possible, use a combination of building blocks (see chapter "Building Blocks").

When there aren't any building blocks, they must be developed. In developing these, many calculations and little experiments should be done to guide the way through.

Some things must be tried to prove the intuitions or preliminary designs (i.e., quick mockups)

32 Calculations

As one becomes experienced, he will do calculations, only where needed, thereby, avoiding analysis paralysis.

If a calculation shows a very small safety factor, don't bother to get exact numbers. It needs to be more robust, i.e. redesigned.

33 Calculations vs Testing

Testing is limited to a small number of lots, whereas calculations or layouts can be made using the known extremes. In this way, robustness can be determined (i.e., windows can be established, and the extremes can show what minimum safety factors are being met). Early in the design process, do conservative approximations and rough calculations to see if you're in the ballpark.

Design Process

Too many calculations and too much detail early on can slow the design process. As the design evolves, some of the earlier ideas are eliminated. Much time is wasted if the designer had done in-depth calculations or got into the fine details before the design has matured. Let the numbers and details guide the design.as matured

34 Your intuition or feel must yield to the numbers.

The more do-loops* done, the closer the feel and intuition comes to the numbers and reality

*do-loops [my definition]: The complete cycle of design, build, use and evaluate

This is very important especially in enhancing your intuition of the real world.

Formulas and physical feel become built-in to one's intuition

35 Things to be wary of

Friction

Wear

Heat

Cold

Strength

Vibration

Design Process

Noise

Size

Corrosion

Weight

Fatigue

Adjustments

Level of precision

Fabrication methods

Assembly

Looks

Aspect ratios

Sealing

Ergonomics Safety

User friendly

Capabilities of people using it

Operator fatigue

Maintenance

Design Process

Cost

Design with these factors always in your mind

36 Apply robust design techniques

When determining design safety factors, one must consider, not only, process loads, but also, fabrication and crash loads. The design must be strong enough to withstand them.

Machining forces, for example, could be much greater than the normal in-use loads.

Minimize thin cross-sections, especially in areas of tight tolerances where machining or in-use loads may compromise fit, form or function.

37 In design, a crucial phase is just after the layout is done and detailing of the parts starts.

At this juncture, one knows more about the project than at any other time. He has gathered much information from his questions, calculations, and other people's input. He has gone through many iterations. This is a time when the most informed decisions can be made. Some of the earlier assumptions may no longer be valid, but the related features were kept. They should be eliminated. Consolidation can happen. This is one way simplification occurs. One cannot be afraid to change things at this late design stage. Don't marry yourself to ideas; time left to complete the project may not allow it. The window of opportunity for the product could be lost. In this situation, the designer may have to unbalance his life and work long

Design Process

hours to raise the level of design to its simplest and best form and still meet deadlines.

If possible, while detailing is being done by others, work on an entirely different project. Flush the mind of the job. When one comes back to it, the job can be looked at with a fresh mind. After detailing, look at the assembly and critique it. Mentally run the device. Will it work flawlessly? Run the mental video under extreme conditions, including maximum and minimum speed, no load and maximum load, minimum and maximum temperatures, etc. Picture the device being used under all conditions.

Picture it at the macroscopic as well as the microscopic level and, at times, down to the molecular level. Do you have a much better idea? You may want to tweak a fit or change a material. Remember, it is easier to change the design on paper or in electronic form than to change it after it is built.

38 Making improvements (changes) late in the process

This is an order of magnitude more difficult, This is an order of magnitude that is more difficult because some parts may have already been made, and other things that interface with that part of the design may have already been committed to.

The art of this is to know when to proceed down the road, or when to cut and go. One can forever tweak or improve the design.

Design Process

When new information arises or a better way is found late in the project, what does one do? If the new idea is much simpler, do it.

Unfortunately, one really starts to learn when building or using the device. Some of the lessons learned are painful. This is why it's so important to use proven systems, the building blocks, whenever possible.

39 The designer must have a sound reason for every detail

Tolerances, finishes, hardnesses, or materials used. When ideas have matured, the designer should talk to the people who will make it, checking fabrication feasibility. He must be able to defend his reasoning for an extremely tight tolerance. It might be stated that it is impossible to make. At this point, the designer must reevaluate his design and be prepared to change it or find another fabrication method or shop that can handle the tolerances.

Keep tolerances as loose as possible while still maintaining proper fit and function. A rule of thumb: Fabrication costs are at least two times greater with tolerances of ±.0005 versus ±.005 [see "Appendix: Cost vs. Tolerance"].

40 Incorporate visual vital signs of the design.

In automatic equipment, have readouts in all the critical areas with alarms as necessary, including pressure, temperature, current, voltage, speed, counts, etc. Design-in sensors vs. adding after the fact. Have capability for graphing and recording readings for troubleshooting or proof that certain parameters are being met. via statistical process control (SPC)

Design Process

"What can be measured can be improved" – Bill Gates

41 Iterations galore

On the way to the final design, the designer must go through many iterations, just like nature. What guide the iterations are calculations, research, experiments, quantum jumps (a brainstorm), punctuated equilibria, new needs, changing requirements, and new information.

Nature's iterations are guided not by calculations or brainstorming but by interfacing with the environment it is in. If some creature is too slow, a predator will wipe it out. Hopefully, the creature can last long enough for a mutation to add a defense mechanism, such as camouflage or quicker leaps. Likewise, mechanical designs must survive the environment they are used in. If they do not perform well, the customer will ask for improvements or eliminate the designs.

Young designers may tend to go with first ideas for many reasons. (It takes too long to come up with better ideas. It has already taken too long to come this far, and the design will probably work.) The designer may feel inadequate because they think that better or more experienced designers don't have to do iterations. The masters do a tremendous number of iterations before the final design is completed.

Rapid prototyping has allowed for more iterations faster, possibly allowing for inadequate pre-engineering. The pressure to get the design right the first time is not there, making for a lazy designer. Build it to see if it works rather

Design Process

than to confirm the design ideas. Pre-engineering may be perceived as not that important—wrong!

There is a natural number of iterations that must take place. If the time limit is too short, the design is not taken to its highest level.

42 Be careful of putting on the blinders too soon, plowing ahead, working on the wrong design and getting wrapped up in its details before the design has gone through the required number of iterations and has evolved to its simplest optimum form.

43 Major flaws

May be found under scrutiny of other engineers, operators or in a design review. It is far better to find the flaws at this stage, before the product is built than failing when put into use.

Operators may not be able to work with the device for the expected output, or it may wear out prematurely. In other words, it fails when it is introduced into its environment. Again, much like nature's designs, failing, because of the environment it's in.

44 Talk with the machinist, mold makers, etc. about how it will be built

Talk to the operators or customers, the people who will use it.

45 Methods of fabrications must be considered to hold tolerances, finishes, etc.

Design Process

46 Make first prototype of a multi station machine as close to the production model as possible.

Incorporate existing building blocks [proven designs] if possible. [see chapter "Building Blocks"]. They must be developed, especially, if they could be used in future machines.

Along the way, during the design process, some things must be tried or experiments run to prove out a theory, concept or intuitions, via quick mockups. Be careful of taking short cuts. If, for example, the coating or hardness of the parts play a large part in the functionality of the concept, then include them in the experiment for more accurate evaluations.

The amount of pre-engineering equals how far one goes up the learning curve on the first shot. [see Appendix: Basic Truths of In- Plant Design] One must engineer the machine to work the first time.

47 Design checklists must be used

There is a good checklist in Machinery's Handbook, by Erik Oberg

Create your own

48 Murphy's Law must be considered Everything that can go wrong will.

O'Toole's Law states that, Murphy was an optimist

49 Specifications

Design Process

Write specifications for tasks to be done inside or outside the company

Forces thought and homework on task to be accomplished. Draws focus on task

Generates constructive criticism from inside and outside sources. Minimizes surprise

50 Drawings and documentation is extremely important

To repeat designs exactly, for replacement of worn, broken or lost parts or to evolve to the next generation, excellent documentation is crucial. Nature uses DNA as a blueprint for its next generation of beings. A good drawing is one that any machinist or engineer throughout the world could understand without asking any questions.

Complete knowledge for manufacture of the part must be given by the drawing so that no further information is necessary. A detail drawing must not be dependent on any other detail. Geometric characteristics and symbols, tolerances, weld symbols, materials, hardness, plating or coating, etc. must be specified as required. Use pictures, icons, symbols and perspectives whenever possible.

Geometric tolerances = icons. Words do not need to be interpreted.

Concentricity, runout, flatness, straightness are intuitive and are directly associated with surfaces with almost no interpretations needed.

Design Process

With CAD producing solid models used in conjunction with CADCAM tools, all dimensions need not be called out. But, critical dimensions with tight tolerances, finishes, hardness's and materials must be denoted, specific information that the geometry by itself, cannot.

Use icons on controls, buttons, manuals, etc. vs words wherever possible. There is nothing better for transferring instruction from one brain to another. Language is taken out of the equation

51 Create Building Blocks [see chapter "Building Blocks"]

When the design includes Building Blocks that have many absolutes imbedded in them, it has a very a high probability of success

52 Strive for perfection, settle for excellence

Building Blocks

Building Blocks

In most companies, there is a critical need for extremely robust building blocks. These building blocks, with their imbedded Six Sigma principles, are machines or processes used to fabricate a company's products. The same principles can be used in designing and making products. The word "absolutes" will be used instead of Six Sigma to foster an intuitive feel. Using building blocks, companies can develop products faster with a high degree of success.

1   Absolutes

    1.1   Demand absolutes. Use as many as possible in the design. Processes must be understood thoroughly and controlled to the nth degree. Depending on the device, the following are some absolutes that might be imbedded

       Self-aligning, or alignment built-in

       Zero play

       Never seizing

       Frictionless

       Never wear

       Never corrode

       Absolute sealing

2   Perfection

Building Blocks

2.1 Striving for perfection helps one develop absolutes and excellent design modules that are added to the repertoire of things in the brain. These can be used over again and again.

2.2 Be careful about perfection. What is a perfect design? Does a perfect design mean providing a design that the customer wants on time? Is it satisfying yourself to the highest degree possible as perceived by you? Does it mean satisfying upper management?

2.3 Strive for perfection, settle for excellence.

3 Excellent Designs

3.1 Save untold money.

3.2 No downtime.

3.3 No time spent in meetings of the highest level (expensive) with people trying to figure what's wrong and how to fix it.

3.4 No rebuilding.

3.5 No scrap and no heavy maintenance.

3.6 Allow efficient use of resources.

3.6.1 Your employee resources can spend their time on new projects vs. correcting mistakes of previous ones.

Building Blocks

4   Especially in a regulated industry, such as the medical field for instance, building blocks are extremely important.

   4.1   Use existing platforms (a form of a building block containing many building blocks) whenever possible. This will save untold hours of work and money while guaranteeing success.

      4.1.1   Saves manufacturing floor space.

   4.2   Don't forget the immense amount of work done to develop machines, processes, and tooling, which include: experimenting, designing, calculating, debugging, process procedures, characteristic studies, protocols, validations, trials, tooling procurement, change orders, and the list goes on.

5   Details are Extremely Important

   5.1   If wrong, they can kill the design. Every tolerance, chamfer, radius, hardness, coating, materials used, etc. are important. Details have the inherent ability to change the course of the design.

6   Time to Complete Projects

   6.1   Should be adequate, factoring in time for unknown issues that will inevitably arise.

   6.2   Quality time to develop the building blocks and absolutes is a must.

   6.3   Overcommitting is a death knell in developing absolutes. Designers should not allow themselves

Building Blocks

to be overcommitted. Management must provide enough resources to complete the job.

6.4 If you could shift just one day of a project with the options to spend that day on details near the end or in the formulation of the design, shift the day to formulation. This would be an attempt to head off working on the wrong thing.

6.5 To deliver excellent designs in a timely manner, one may need to ask for help.

    6.5.1 To speed up the project, have documentation, drawings, and detailing done by others.

    6.5.2 If needed, have finite element analysis (FEA) done by others.

    6.5.3 Subdivide tasks and transfer them to others.

    6.5.4 Have experiments done by others.

    6.5.5 Have testing done by others.

7 Modular Design

7.1 Modular design is very important and is to be utilized whenever possible. Subassemblies or stations of semiautomatic or automatic machines, as far as practical, should be self- contained units that could be run offline without being connected to the main (host) machine in any way. The station would have its own frame and no external devices acting on or influencing the module. Mechanical alignment of

Building Blocks

the components within the module should not be dependent on host machine; however, alignment to the host machine must be addressed. It would include its own pneumatic and electrical system. It must have the capability to be run in a manual or automatic mode. Modular design allows for parallel efforts in a group of engineers working on a project. It's up to the project engineer to make sure all design modules will meld together.

7.2 Modules can be built by outside sources without knowing the whole picture. This is important when secrecy is necessary.

7.3 The modules can be used as part of an automatic machine as well as an operator-dependent station in a work cell.

8 Vital Signs of the Design

8.1 Equipment should have readouts in all the critical areas.

8.2 Utilize air cylinders versus springs where adjustability. Flexibility is important. Where pressure gages provide a vital readout.

8.3 Temperature readouts for processes

9 Design Characteristics and Things to Be Wary Of (see Design Process, Item 35)

Looks good Robust design High functionality Reliability Simplicity

Building Blocks

10 Machine Shops

10.1 For critical jobs with tight tolerances, hardnesses, and finishes, use only those with quality control and shop floor control. If they do military work, that's a plus, proving that they can meet critical criteria. For quick and low tolerance stuff, use a small shop with low overhead. For competitive bidding, it is only fair to use equivalent shops.

10.2 Each shop will win their fair share. No games will be played. They learn to give you their very best quote first because they don't get a second chance. Take the low bidder and ask him if they can cut the cost. Where has the price been increased because of risk of making the part? Maybe the designer can loosen up a tolerance or make a change in the design to lower the cost.

Zone

Zone

When a designer starts to work on a design, he must enter the Zone. In this mode, he brings to bear multiple areas of the brain.

1   Criteria of being in the Zone No sense of time.

   Dancing with the creative spirit

   Totally in tune with visualization and computer interactions.

   Startled if interrupted

   Focused effort = entering and staying in the Zone.

   No distractions

2   While in the Zone, one recalls directories and files that will relate to the design and start to create combinations. An analogy: A flower's roots get nourishment from minerals in the ground to create a beautiful blossom.

3   In the Zone, the designer is in his own world with cascading thoughts flourishing

4   Visualization [running a mental video of the design in your head] can only happen while in the Zone

5   Having fun, dancing with the creative spirit and enhancing the elegance of the design. "Artists feel that something holy is going on when they paint, that there is something in the act of creating which is like a religious revelation." [May, Rollo (1994). The Courage to Create. p 69) New York: W. W. Norton & Co.]

Zone

6   When working on a complex design and something pops up in your mind that needs to be checked out or remembered, but, it's not directly related to the design at hand, write it down so it can be dealt with later, when outside the zone. This allows for continuity of thought while in the Zone, the picture remaining clear.

7   While in the Zone, you are mentally building the machine or device before applying the CAD tools. The pictures become clearer, like a camera focusing. An analogy: Magic Eye 3-D pictures: As one stares at the page, a three-dimensional image starts to emerge and becomes clear, but with a slight movement of the eyes or a distraction, the image is gone and must be reestablished. To experience this phenomenon, a free Android app can be downloaded to your smartphone, 3D Magic Eye by Huesoft [iPhone should have an equivalent]. In the real world, distractions or interruptions of any kind collapse that mental image. Cell phones, etc. should be set aside, out of reach, when one is trying to concentrate.

8   While in the Zone, one becomes unaware of where he is or what time it is. It has been said that Einstein was a social imbecile while totally absolved in thought, with unmatched socks, who didn't know where he was or what time it was.

9   One must question all the answers that come to you while in the Zone. They are not perfect and often need iterations.

10 One enters the Zone and begins a heavily concentrated design effort for a long period of time. This naturally creates mind inertia. The design thoughts carry on even after one has, apparently, stopped working on the design.

Zone

An analogy: A heavy, high-inertia object has a force acting on it. The longer the force is applied, the faster the object goes and the longer it will stay in motion after the force is removed. These thoughts are shifted to the subconscious, and mind inertia keeps them alive. The subconscious mind is nonjudgmental and automatically organizes thoughts and places them in the appropriate directories. Plus, it has access to information that has unknowingly been stored, information that has been gathered over a lifetime that is not readily accessible to the conscious mind. That's why while driving home, relaxing, spending time with the family, in the shower, or at 3:00 in the morning, an idea pops into your head, an idea that may not have germinated if you were still in the zone wrapped up in the details. These ideas cannot be totally trusted. They are not to scale and must survive the scrutiny of supporting calculations, layouts, etc. It may be just another iteration of the design, or it could be an epiphany that starts one on an entirely new path.

11 One must learn to enter the Zone and exit it. If one is in the Zone too long, family, friends and your balance suffer [see Balance in the Chapter: Epilogue]

12 While in the Zone, ask a question and the mind starts working on it. Many times, the answer comes. An analogy: Pray for something, your mind starts working on it and it happens, i.e., your prayers are answered

13 In the book, Courage to Create, by Rollo May, Chapter Two, in paragraph 'Intensity of the Encounter' he describes being in the Zone very aptly.

Zone

"This leads us to the second element in the creative act— namely, the intensity of the encounter. Absorption, being caught up in, wholly involved, and so on, are used commonly to describe the state of the artist or scientist when creating or even the child at play. By whatever name one calls it, genuine creativity is characterized by an intensity of awareness, a heightened consciousness.

Artists, as well as you and I in moments of intensive encounter, experience quite clear neurological changes. These include quickened heart beat; higher blood pressure; increased intensity and constriction of vision, with eyelids narrowed so that we can see more vividly the scene we are painting; we become oblivious to things around us (as well as to the passage of time). We experience a lessening of appetite— persons engaged in a creative act lose interest in eating at the moment, and may work right through mealtime without noticing it. Now all of these correspond to an inhibiting of the functioning of the parasympathetic division of the autonomic nervous system (which has to do with ease, comfort, nourishment) and an activation of the sympathetic nervous division. And, lo and behold, we have the same picture that Walter B. Cannon described as the "flight- fight" mechanism, the energizing of the organism for fighting or fleeing. This is the neurological correlate of what we find, in broad terms, in anxiety and fear.

But what the artist or creative scientist feels is not anxiety or fear; it is joy. I use the word in contrast to happiness or pleasure. The artist, at the moment of creating, does not experience gratification or satisfaction (though this may be the case later, after he or she has a highball or a pipe in the evening. Rather, it is joy, joy defined as the emotion

Zone

that goes with heightened consciousness, the mood that accompanies the experience of actualizing one's own potentialities.

Now this intensity of awareness is not necessarily connected with conscious purpose or willing. It may occur in reverie or in dreams, or from so-called unconscious levels. An eminent New York professor related an illustrative story. He had been searching for a particular chemical formula for some time, but without success. One night, while he was sleeping, he had a dream in which the formula was worked out and displayed before him. He woke up, and in the darkness, he excitedly wrote it down on a piece of tissue, the only thing he could find. But the next morning he could not read his own scribbling. Every night thereafter, upon going to bed, he would concentrate his hopes on dreaming the dream again. Fortunately, after some nights he did, and he then wrote the formula down for good.

It was the formula he had sought and for which he received the Nobel prize.

Though not rewarded so dramatically, we have all had similar experiences. Processes of forming, making, building go on even if we are not consciously aware of them at the time.

William James once said that we learn to swim in the winter and to skate in the summer.

Whether you wish to interpret these phenomena in terms of some formulation of the unconscious, or prefer to follow William James in connecting them with some neurological

Zone

processes that continue even when we are not working on them, or prefer some other approach, as I do, it is still clear that creativity goes on in varying degrees of intensity on levels not directly under the control of conscious willing. Hence the heightened awareness we are speaking of does not at all mean increased self-consciousness. It is rather correlated with abandon and absorption, and it involves a heightening of awareness in the whole personality.

But let it be said immediately that unconscious insights or answers to problems that come in reverie do not come hit or miss. They may indeed occur at times of relaxation, or in fantasy, or at other times when we alternate play with work. But what is entirely clear is that they pertain to those areas in which the person consciously has worked laboriously and with dedication. Purpose in the human being is a much more complex phenomenon than what used to be called will power. Purpose involves all levels of experience. We cannot will to have insights. We cannot will creativity. But we can will to give ourselves to the encounter with intensity of dedication and commitment. The deeper aspects of awareness are activated to the extent that the person is committed to the encounter.

We must also point out that this "intensity of encounter" is not to be identified with what is called the Dionysian aspect of creativity. You will find this word Dionysian used often in books on creative works. Taken from the name of the Greek god of intoxication and other forms of ecstasy, the term refers to the upsurge of vitality, the abandon, which characterized the ancient orgiastic revels of Dionysus.

Zone

Nietzsche, in his important book The Birth of Tragedy, cites the Dionysian principle of surging vitality and the Apollonian principle of form and rational order as the two dialectical principles that operate in creativity. This dichotomy is assumed by many students and writers.

The Dionysian aspect of intensity can be studied psychoanalytically easily enough. Probably almost every artist has tried at some time or other to paint while under the influence of alcohol. What happens generally is what one would expect, and it happens in proportion to how much alcohol is consumed— namely, that the artist thinks he or she is doing wonderful stuff, indeed much better than usual, but in actual fact, as is noted the next morning while looking at the picture, has really performed less well than usual. Certainly, Dionysian periods of abandon are valuable, particularly in our mechanized civilization where creativity and the arts are all but starved to death by the routine of punching clocks and attending endless committee meetings, and by the pressures to produce ever greater quantities of papers and books, pressures that have infested the academic world more lethally than the industrial world. I long for the health-giving effects of the periods of "carnival," such as they still have in the Mediterranean countries.

But the intensity of the creative act should be related to the encounter objectively, and not released merely by something the artist "takes." Alcohol is a depressant, and possibly necessary in an industrial civilization; but when one needs it regularly to feel free of inhibitions, he or she is misnaming the problem. The issue really is why the inhibitions are there in the first place. The psychological studies of the upsurge of vitality and other effects

Zone

that occur when such drugs are taken are exceedingly interesting; but one must sharply distinguish this from the intensity that accompanies the encounter itself. The encounter is not something that occurs merely because we ourselves have subjectively changed; it represents, rather, a real relationship with the objective world.

The important and profound aspect of the Dionysian principle is that of ecstasy. It was in connection with Dionysian revels that Greek drama was developed, a magnificent summit of creativity which achieved a union of form and passion with order and vitality. Ecstasy is the technical term for the process in which this union occurs. The topic of ecstasy is one to which we should give more active attention in psychology. I use the word, of course, not in its popular and cheapened sense of "hysteria," but in its historical, etymological sense of "ex-stasis"— that is, literally to "stand out from," to be freed from the usual split between subject and object which is a perpetual dichotomy in most human activity. Ecstasy is the accurate term for the intensity of consciousness that occurs in the creative act. But it is not to be thought of merely as a Bacchic "letting go"; it involves the total person, with the subconscious and unconscious acting in unity with the conscious. It is not, thus, irrational; it is, rather, suprarational. It brings intellectual, volitional, and emotional functions into play all together.

What I am saying may sound strange in the light of our traditional academic psychology. It should sound strange. Our traditional psychology has been founded on the dichotomy between subject and object which has been the central characteristic of Western thought for the past four centuries. Ludwig Binswanger calls this dichotomy

Zone

"the cancer of all psychology and psychiatry up to now."
It is not avoided by behaviorism or operationalism, which
would define experience only in objective terms. Nor is it
avoided by isolating the creative experience as a purely
subjective phenomenon.

Most psychological and other modern schools of thought
still assume this split without being aware of it. We have
tended to set reason over against emotions, and have
assumed, as an outgrowth of this dichotomy, that we could
observe something most accurately if our emotions were
not involved— that is to say, we would be least biased if
we had no emotional stake at all in the matter at hand.
I think this is an egregious error. There are now data
in Rorschach responses, for example, that indicate that
people can more accurately observe precisely when they
are emotionally involved— that is, reason works better
when emotions are present; the person sees sharper and
more accurately when his emotions are engaged.

Indeed, we really see an object unless we have some
emotional involvement with it. It may well be that reason
works best in the state of ecstasy.

The Dionysian and the Apollonian must be related to
each other. Dionysian vitality rests on this question:
What manner of encounter releases the vitality? What
particular relation to landscape or inner vision or idea
heightens the consciousness, brings forth the intensity?"

[May, Rollo (1994). The Courage to Create. (pp. 44-50)
New York: W. W. Norton & Co.]

Zone

14 The Zone phenomena can be experienced by people in other fields, i.e. athletes, musicians, scientists, actors, dancers, singers, writers and composers

    14.1 Bill Russell, best defensive center in NBA history. Won eleven NBA and two NCAA championships.

    In his biography, Bill Russell describes those moments [being in the zone] as one of an almost supernatural intuition. "It was almost as though we were playing in slow motion. During those spells, I could almost sense how the next play would develop and the next shot would be taken. Even before the other team brought the ball inbounds, I could feel it so keenly....."

    14.2 In the book, 10% Happier by Dan Harris, he talks about focusing on the task at hand.

    "So you're telling me that I can't multitask?" I asked as we sat down for an interview. "It's not me telling you," she said. "It's neuroscience that would say that our capacity to multitask is virtually nonexistent. Multitasking is a computer-derived term. We have one processor. We can't do it." "I think that when I'm sitting at my desk feverishly doing seventeen things at once that I'm being clever and efficient, but you're saying I'm actually wasting my time?" "Yes, because when you're moving from this project to that project, your mind flits back to the original project, and it can't pick it up where it left off. So it has to take a few steps back and then ramp up again, and that's where the productivity loss is." This problem was, of course, exacerbated in the age of

Zone

what had been dubbed the "info-blitzkrieg," where it took superhuman strength to ignore the siren call of the latest tweet, or the blinking red light on the BlackBerry. Scientists had even come up with a term for this condition: "continuous partial attention." It was a syndrome with which I was intimately familiar, even after all my meditating.

Marturano recommended something radical: do only one thing at a time. When you're on the phone, be on the phone. When you're in a meeting, be there. Set aside an hour to check your email, and then shut off your computer monitor and focus on the task at hand."

[Harris, Dan (2014). 10% Happier (pp. 172-173) New York: HarperCollins Publishers]

Creativity

Creativity

Creativity is a mystical, magical wizardry. A driving force imbedded in the brain's inner sanctum where it all happens: searching the internal files (stored information) and using it to create, optimize, combine and iterate; thereby, changing the design path toward new designs.

Creativity is a crucial part of the design process. It is a key element in many fields of endeavor. Whether it be machine design, finance, architecture, marketing and virtually all of the arts. It guides one through the evolutionary/iterative process of designing/creating something. Creativity is a form of mental gyrations, engaging the conscious and subconscious mind [both sides, front and back of the brain] drawing from knowledge, logic, imagination and intuition to see connections and distinctions between ideas and things.

1   Dr. Sidney Parnes, as described by Father Camillus Barth, likens the work of creative imagination to the use of a kaleidoscope.

Just as we form new designs by manipulating the particles we see in the kaleidoscope, so we form new ideas by manipulating the details. The more particles in a kaleidoscope the more new designs; the more facts, observations and abstractions in our minds, the more new insights into the mysteries of intuitive cognition and the more new ideas. Much of the creative behavior is the result of drive-coupling the imagination with intent, effort and courage.

2   Below is a summarization of Mihaly Csikszentmihaly's work put together by Theodore Lucas, Managing Partner, Chairman of the Investment Committee of Lattice Strategies an investment firm. I thought Lucas,

Creativity

eloquently, captured the essence of Csikszentmihaly's work in a condensed form. It aligned well with what I experienced throughout my career. Some of his phrases noted by quotation marks aligned with points made in this book are denoted by brackets:

"great concentration" [in the Zone]

"intellectually brilliant can actually be detrimental to creativity" [blinded by brilliance]

"on the shoulders of giants" [stand on the shoulders of giants]

"humble and confident at the same time"

[must be humble to receive new learnings]

"very passionate about their work" [must have a passion for it]

"Yet over and over again, the importance of seeing people, hearing people, exchanging ideas and getting to know another person's work and mind are stressed by creative individuals." [The designer must keep communicating with all levels of people ... Brainstorming can be an important tool in design ... Talk with the machinist, mold makers ... Talk to the operators or customers]

"Yet when the person is working in the area of his or her expertise, worries and cares fall away, replaced by a sense of bliss" [dancing with the creative spirit] ["artists feel that something holy is going on when they paint

Creativity

...... Ecstasy is the accurate term for the intensity of consciousness that occurs in the creative act." Rolo May]

"Mihaly Csikszentmihaly, formerly chairman of the psychology department at the University of Chicago, is considered to be one of the leading researchers of the subject of human creativity. His book, Creativity, summarizes thirty years of study and extensive interaction with a large body of "creators" across a variety of disciplines.

Csikszentmihaly (refer to him as "MC") begins the book by stating the centrality of creativity to human existence, arguing that it is both a central source of meaning in our lives and when we are involved in creative acts, we feel we are living more fully than during the rest of life. In defining creativity, he states that it is "any act, idea or product that changes an existing domain, or that transforms an existing domain into a new one." Very often, creativity involves combining or synthesizing existing elements into something novel and having greater value than the sum of the parts individually. The Attributes of Creative Contributors in Creativity, MC goes on to profile a wide array of recognized creators in an attempt to define what makes up a creative personality. Before summarizing what he concludes to be the ten defining characteristics of creative individuals, he notes that an overarching point of definition is that they are "remarkable for their ability to adapt to almost any situation and to make do with whatever is at hand to reach their goals." A patched together excerpt summary of the nine defining characteristics of creativity according to MC follows below:"

"Creative individuals have a great deal of physical energy, but they are also often quiet and at rest. They work long

Creativity

hours, with great concentration, while projecting an aura of freshness and enthusiasm. .... It seems that the energy of [creative people] is internally generated due more to their focused minds than to the superiority of their genes. ....

This does not mean that that creative persons are hyperactive, always 'on,' constantly churning away. In fact, they often take rests and sleep a lot. The important thing is that the energy is under their own control – it is not controlled by a calendar, the clock or an external schedule. When necessary they can focus it like a laser beam; when it is not, they immediately start recharging their batteries. They consider the rhythm of activity followed by idleness or reflection very important for the success of their work.

Creative individuals tend to be smart, yet also naïve at the same time. How smart they are is actually open to question. .... The earliest longitudinal study of superior mental abilities, initiated at Stanford University by the psychologist Lewis Terman in 1921, shows rather conclusively that children with very high IQs do well in life, but after a certain point IQ does not seem to be correlated with superior performance in real life. Later studies suggest that the cutoff point is around 120; it might be difficult to do creative work with a lower IQ, but beyond 120 and increment in IQ does not necessarily imply higher creativity. Why a low intelligence interferes with creative accomplishment is quite obvious. But being intellectually brilliant can also be detrimental to creativity. Some people with high IQs get complacent, and, secure in their mental superiority, they lose the curiosity essential to achieving anything new.

Creativity

Learning facts, playing by the existing rules of domains, may come so easily to a high-IQ person that he or she never has any incentive to question, doubt and improve on existing knowledge. This is probably why Goethe, among others, said naïveté is the most important attribute of a genius. ....

Furthermore, people who bring about acceptable novelty in a domain seem able to use well two opposite ways of thinking: the convergent and the divergent. Convergent thinking is measured by IQ tests, and it involves solving well defined, rational problems that have one correct answer.

Divergent thinking leads to no agreed upon solution. It involves fluency, or the ability to generate a great quantity of ideas; flexibility, or the ability to switch from one perspective to another; and originality in picking unusual associations of ideas. .... Divergent thinking is not much use without the ability to   tell a good idea from a bad one – and this selectivity involves convergent thinking.

Manfred Eigen is one of several scientists who claim that the only difference between them and their less creative colleagues is that they can tell whether a problem is soluble or not, and this saves enormous amounts of time and many false starts.

George Stigler stresses the importance of fluidity that is divergent thinking on one hand, and good judgment in recognizing a viable problem on the other. 3. A third paradoxical trait refers to the related combination of playfulness and discipline. There is no question that a playfully light attitude is typical of creative individuals.

Creativity

.... But this playfulness doesn't go very far without its antithesis, a quality of doggedness, endurance, perseverance. Much hard work is necessary to bring a novel idea to completion and to surmount the obstacles a creative person inevitably encounters. .... Despite the carefree air that many creative people affect, most of them work late into the night and persist when less driven individuals would not.

Creative individuals alternate between imagination at one end, and a rooted sense of reality at the other. Both are needed to break away from the present without losing touch with the past. Albert Einstein once wrote that art and science are two of the greatest forms of escape from reality that humans have devised. In a sense he was right: Great art and great science involve a leap of imagination into a world that is different from the present. The rest of society often views these new ideas as fantasies without relevance to current reality. And they are right. But the whole point of art and science is to go beyond what we now consider real, and create a new reality. At the same time, this 'escape' is not into a never-never land. What makes a novel idea creative is that once we see it, sooner or later we recognize that, strange as it is, it is true. Most of us assume that artists – musicians, writers, poets, painters – are strong on the fantasy side, whereas scientists, politicians and businesspeople are realists. This may be true in terms of day-to-day routine activities. But when a person begins to work creatively, all bets are off – the artist may be as much a realist as the physicist, and the physicist as imaginative as the artist.

Creative people tend to harbor opposite tendencies on the continuum between extroversions and introversion.

Creativity

Usually each of us tends to be one or the other, either preferring to be in the thick of crowds or sitting on the sidelines and observing the passing show. In fact, in current psychological research, extroversion and introversion are considered the most stable personality traits that differentiate people from each other and that can be reliably measured. Creative individuals, on the other hand, seem to express both traits at the same time. The stereotype of the 'solitary genius' is strong and gets ample support from our interviews. After all, one must generally be alone in order to write, paint or do experiments in a laboratory. As we know from studies of young talented people, teenagers who cannot stand being alone tend not to develop their skills because practicing music or studying math requires a solitude they dread. Only those teens who can tolerate being alone are able to master the symbolic content of a domain. Yet over and over again, the importance of seeing people, hearing people, exchanging ideas and getting to know another person's work and mind are stressed by creative individuals. The physicist John Wheeler expresses this point with his usual directness: 'If you don't kick things around with people, you are out of it. Nobody, I always say, can be anybody without somebody being around.'

Creative individuals are remarkably humble and confident at the same time. It is remarkable to meet a [great creator] whom you expect to be arrogant or supercilious, only to encounter self-deprecation and shyness instead. Yet there are good reasons why this should be so. In the first place, these individuals are aware that they stand, in Newton's words, 'on the shoulders of giants.' Their respect for the domain in which they work makes them aware of the long

Creativity

line of previous contributions to it, which puts their own into perspective.

Second, they are also aware of the role that luck played in their achievements. And, third, they are usually so focused on future projects and current challenges that their past accomplishments, no matter how outstanding, are no longer very interesting to them. Another way of expressing this duality is to see it as a contrast between ambition and selflessness, or competition and cooperation. It is often necessary for creative individuals to be ambitious and aggressive. Yet at the same time, they are also willing to subordinate their own personal comfort and advancement to the success of whatever project they are working on.

Generally, creative people are thought to be rebellious and independent. Yet it is impossible to be creative without having internalized a domain of culture. And a person must believe in the importance of such a domain in order to learn its rules; hence he or she must be to an extent a traditionalist. So, it is difficult to see how a person can be creative without being both traditional and conservative and at the same time being rebellious and iconoclastic. Being only traditional leaves the domain unchanged; constantly taking chances without regard to what has been valued in the past rarely leads to novelty that is accepted as an improvement. But the willingness to take risks, to break with the safety of tradition, is also necessary.

Most creative people are very passionate about their work, yet they can be extremely objective about it as well. The energy generated by this conflict between attachment

Creativity

and detachment has been mentioned by many as being an important part of their work. Without the passion, we soon lose interest in a difficult task. Yet without being objective about it, our work is not very good and lacks credibility.

Finally, the openness and sensitivity of creative individuals often exposes them to suffering yet also a great deal of enjoyment. The suffering is easy to understand. The greater sensitivity can cause slights and anxieties that are not usually felt by the rest of us: 'Inventors have a low threshold of pain. Things bother them.' Being alone at the forefront of a discipline also makes you exposed and vulnerable. Eminence invites criticism and attacks. Divergent thinking is often perceived as deviant by the majority, and so the creative person may feel isolated and misunderstood. Yet when the person is working in the area of his or her expertise, worries and cares fall away, replaced by a sense of bliss. Perhaps the most important quality, the one that is most consistently present in all creative individuals, is the ability to enjoy the process of creation for its own sake." MC ends his explanation of the nine traits with the caveat that the list is to a certain extent arbitrary – there are other traits that could be considered important that have been left out and a person can be creative without exhibiting all the dimensions on his list. But he says that the underlying theme is the existence of conflicting traits in the same person.

Without the first pole, new ideas will not be recognized; without the second pole, they will not be developed to the point of acceptance. In conclusion, he says: "The novelty that survives to change a domain is usually the work of

Creativity

someone who can operate at both ends of these polarities – and that is the kind of person we call 'creative.'"

Ted Lucas Lattice Strategies APPLIED RISK STRATEGY January 27, 2014 Critical Investment Challenges and Creativity

3   The Creative Spirit

[from 'The Creative Spirit' by Daniel Goleman, Paul Kaufman, Michael Ray]

"PAVING THE WAY"

"The first stage is preparation, when you immerse yourself in the problem, searching out any information that might be relevant. It's when you let your imagination roam free, open yourself to anything that is even vaguely relevant to the problem. The idea is to gather a broad range of data so that unusual and unlikely elements can begin to juxtapose themselves. Being receptive, being able to listen openly and well, is a crucial skill here.

That's easier said than done. We are used to our mundane way of thinking about solutions. Psychologists call the trap of the routine "functional fixedness": we see only the obvious way of looking at a problem-- the same comfortable way we always think about it. The result is sometimes a jokingly   called psychosclerosis" -- hardening of the attitudes.

Another barrier to taking in fresh information is self-censorship that inner voice of judgment that confines our creative spirit within the boundaries of what we deem

Creativity

acceptable. It's the voice of judgement that whispers to you, "They'll think I'm foolish," "That will never work," "That's too obvious."

We can learn to recognize this voice of judgment, and have the courage to discount its destructive advice. Remind yourself of what Mark Twain once said: "The man with a new idea is a crank until the idea succeeds. To the stage of preparation, we can add another, which, because it's very uncomfortable, is often overlooked: frustration. Frustration arises at the point when the rational, analytic mind, searching laboriously for a solution, reaches the limit of its abilities. Says Stanford's Jim Collins, who teaches creativity to some of the world's best young businesspeople, "If you talk to people who have done really creative things, they'll tell you about the long hours, the anguish, the frustration, all the preparation before something clicks and bam! you move forward with a great leap. But they can't make a great leap without working their brains out."

Although no one enjoys frustration and despair, people who sustain their creativity over the course of a lifetime do come to accept periods of anguish as necessary parts of the whole creative process. Accepting that there is an inevitable "darkness before the dawn" helps in several ways, When the darkness is seen as a necessary prelude to the creative light, one is less likely to ascribe frustration to personal inadequacy or label it "bad." This more positive view of anxiety can foster a greater willingness to persist in trying to solve a problem, in spite of the frustration. Since evidence suggests that people often fail in trying to solve problems not because the problems are insoluble but because they give up prematurely, persistence can be seen

Creativity

as one of our greatest allies. However, there often comes a   point when the wisest course of action is to cease all effort. At this moment, the rational mind surrenders to the problem." [pp. 18-19]

"INCUBATION"

"Once you have mulled over all the relevant pieces and pushed your rational mind to the limits, you can let the problem simmer. This is the incubation stage, when you digest all you have gathered. Whereas preparation demands active work, incubation is more passive, a stage when much of what goes on occurs outside your focused awareness, in the mind's unconscious. As the saying goes, you "sleep on it."

Although you may pluck the problem from this mental twilight zone from time to time and devote your full attention to it, your mind continues to seek a solution whether or not you are consciously thinking about the problem. Indeed, the answer may come to you in a dream, or in that dreamlike state as you are on the verge of sleep, or on first awakening in the morning.

We often underestimate the power of the unconscious mind. But it is far more suited to a creative insight than is the conscious mind. There are no self-censoring judgments in the unconscious, where ideas are free to recombine with other ideas in novel patterns and unpredictable association in a kind of promiscuous fluidity.

Another strength of the unconscious mind is that it is the storehouse of everything you know, including things you can't readily call into awareness. Cognitive scientists,

Creativity

who study how information flows through the brain, tell us that all memory is unconscious before it becomes conscious, and that only a very small fraction of what the mind takes in—less than one percent—ever reaches conscious awareness. In this sense, the unconscious mind is intellectually richer than the conscious part of the mind: it has more data from which to draw upon.

Further, the unconscious speaks to us in ways that go beyond words. What the unconscious mind knows includes the deep feelings and rich imagery that constitutes the intelligence of the senses. What the unconscious mind knows is often more apparent as a felt sense of correctness— a hunch. We call this kind of knowing intuition.

Our intuition draws directly on the vast storehouse of information which is an open book to the unconscious, but to some degree closed to consciousness. That is why, for instance, courses preparing students to take the Scholastic Aptitude Test advise that if we are stumped by a question, we should make as our guess the first answer that seems right. Indeed, experimental studies have found that people's first hunches generally form the basis for better decisions than those decisions made after rationally working through the pros and cons. When we trust our intuition, we are really turning to the wisdom of the unconscious." [pp. 19-20]

"PERCHANCE TO DAYDREAM"

"We are more open to insights from the unconscious mind in moments of reverie, when we are not thinking of anything in particular. That is why daydreams are so

Creativity

useful in the quest for creativity. The fruitfulness of first immersing yourself in a problem, then setting it aside for a while, jibes with the experience of Paul MacCready, an inventor who has tackled creative challenges such as building a human- powered airplane. "You have to get yourself immersed in the subject, and to a certain extent you need some good technical preparation in order to get started," says MacCready. "Then, if it gets interesting to you, you start thinking about it at odd hours. Maybe you can't come up with a solution, and you forget about it for a while, and suddenly while you're shaving you get a good idea."

Shaving is one of MacCready's most creative times: "You have to concentrate just enough so there aren't too many distractions, and you often find yourself thinking of wildly different subjects and coming up with solutions to some of the day's challenges or some of the big projects you are dealing with."

Anytime you can just daydream and relax is useful in the creative process: a shower, long drives, a quiet walk. For example, Nolan Bushnell, the founder of the Atari company, got the inspiration for what became a best-selling video game while idly flicking sand on a beach.

"The only big ideas I've ever had, have come from daydreaming, but modern life seems intent on keeping people from daydreaming,"

Paul MacCready adds. "Every moment of the day your mind is being occupied, controlled, by someone else. At school, at work, watching television—it's somebody else's mind controlling what you think about.

Creativity

Getting away from all that is really important. You need to kick back in a chair or get in a car without having the radio on— and just let your mind daydream."[pp. 21-22]

BIG C AND LITTLE c

Still, much of what we know about our subject comes from the study of the creative giants. Howard Gardner has studied creative geniuses working early in this century, and notes: "The amazing thing about Albert Einstein, or Sigmund Freud, or Virginia Woolf, or Martha Graham, is that they didn't just do something new. They actually changed the field or domain in which they worked forever after. But absent an initial curiosity and passion, which every one of these people had from an early age, and absent years of commitment, when they really took dancing or painting or physics or statesmanship as far as other people had, they would never have had the kind of creative breakthrough that changes a whole field."

Gardner believes that what is true about the Big C creators holds for the rest of us. Each of us. Each of us has a bent for a particular domain. "Every person has certain areas in which he or she has a special interest," says Gardner. "It could be something they do at work—the way they write memos or their craftsmanship at a factory—or the way they teach a lesson or sell something. After working for a while they can get to be pretty good—as good as anybody whom they know in their immediate world.

"Now, many people are satisfied at just being good, but I wouldn't use the word creative to describe this level of work."

Creativity

However, there are others for whom simply being good at something is not enough—they need to be creative. "They can't get into flow when they're just doing things in a routine way," Gardner explains. "So, what they do is to set small challenges for themselves, like making a meal a little different." [pp. 27-29]

CREATIVITY STEW

Daily life is a major arena for innovation and problem-solving—the largest but least honored realm of the creative spirit. As Freud said, two hallmarks of a healthy life are the abilities to love and to work. Each requires imagination

Being creative is kind of like making a stew," says Teresa Amabile. There are three basic kinds of things a stew needs to be really good."

The essential ingredient, something like the vegetables or the meat in a stew, is expertise in a specific area: domain skills. These skills represent your basic mastery of a field. To possess these skills means that you know how to write musical notation, how to skillfully use a computer graphics program, or how to do scientific experiments.

"No one is going to do anything creative in nuclear physics unless that person knows something—and probably a great deal—about nuclear physics," Amabile observes. "In the same way an artist isn't going to be creative unless that person has the technical skills required for, say, making etchings or mixing colors. The ingredients of creativity start with skill in the domain—with the expertise

Creativity

Many people have a flair for something. "Talent is the natural propensity for being able to produce great work in a particular domain," says Amabile. "For example, it's highly unlikely that, given the kind of musical training that Mozart was given, just any child could end up producing the work that Mozart produced. There was something Mozart had from the start that made it easy for him to listen to music, to understand it, and be able to produce so much, so well, at such an early age."

But without training in the skills of a domain, even the most promising talent will languish. And with proper skill development, even an average talent can become the basis for creativity.

The second ingredient in the stew is what Amabile calls "creative thinking skills": ways of approaching the world that allow you to find a novel possibility and see it through to full execution. "These are like the spices and herbs you use to bring out the flavor of the basic ingredients in a stew," Amabile says. "They make the flavors unique, help the basic ingredients to blend and bring out something different."

These creative thinking skills, include being able to imagine a diverse range of possibilities, being persistent in tackling a problem, and having high standards for work. "They also include the ability to turn things over in your mind, like trying to make the strange familiar and the familiar strange," Amabile adds. "Many of these skills have to do with being an independent person: being willing to take risks and having the courage to try something you've never done before."

Creativity

Another variety of these skills has to do with sensing how to nurture the creative process itself, such as knowing when to let go of a problem and allow it to incubate for a while. If a person has only technical skills in a field—the first ingredient—but no creative thinking skills, the stew will turn out flat and flavorless.

Finally, the element that really cooks the creative stew is passion. The psychological term is intrinsic motivation, the urge to do something for the sheer pleasure of doing it rather than for any prize or compensation.

The opposite kind of motivation—extrinsic— makes you do something not because you want to, but because you ought to. You do it for a reward, to please someone, or to get a good evaluation.

Creativity begins to cook when people are motivated by the pure enjoyment of what they are doing. A Nobel Prize-winning physicist, Amabile recalls, was asked what he thought made the difference between creative and uncreative scientists. He said it was whether or not their work was "a labor of love."

The most successful, groundbreaking scientists are not always the most gifted, but the ones who are impelled by a driving curiosity. To some degree a strong passion can make up for a lack of raw talent. Passion "is like the fire underneath the soup pot," Amabile says. " It really heats everything up, blends the flavors, and makes those spices mix with the basic ingredients to produce something that tastes wonderful."[pp. 29-31]

AFFINITY AND PERSISTENCE

Creativity

Creativity begins with an affinity for something. It's like falling in love. "The most important thing at the beginning is for an individual to feel some kind of emotional connection to something," says Howard Gardner.

Albert Einstein's fascination with physics began when he was just five, when he was ill in bed. His father brought him a present—a small magnetic compass. For hours, Einstein lay in bed, entranced by the needle that infallibly pointed the way north. When he was close to seventy, Einstein said, "This experience made a deep and lasting impression on me. Something deeply hidden had to be behind things."

Gardner believes such childhood moments are one key to understanding creative lives. "Without that initial love and emotional connection, I think that the chances of doing good creative work later on are minimal," Gardner says. "But the initial intoxication is not enough in itself. It essentially moves you to take steps to learn more about the thing that first interests you, and to discover its complexities, its difficulties, its strengths and obscurities."

From that initial love of doing something comes persistence. People who care passionately about what they are doing don't give up easily. When frustration comes, they persist. When people are resistant to their innovation, they keep going anyway, As Thomas Edison said, "Sticking to it is the genius!"

Deaf and blind, Helen Keller was cut off from the world and human contact until Anne Sullivan came along. Sullivan's creativity lay in her passion and her refusal to

Creativity

give up. She was willing to persist in her determination to reach Helen.

Years later, Helen Keller recalled that first moment when that persistence, love, and passion bore fruit:

"My teacher Anne Mansfield Sullivan had been with me nearly a month, and she taught me the names of a number of objects. She would put them into my hand, spelled out their names with her fingers, and helped me to form the letters.

"But I didn't have the faintest idea of what she was doing. I do not know what I thought. I have only a tactile memory of my fingers going through those motions and changing from one position to another.

"One day she handed me a cup and spelled the word. Then she poured some liquid into the cup and spelled the letters: W-A-T-E-R.

"She says I looked puzzled. I was confusing the two words, spelling cup for water and water for cup.

"Finally I became angry because Miss Sullivan kept repeating the words over and over. In despair she led me out to the ivy- covered pump house and made me hold the cup under the spout while she pumped.

"In her other hand she spelled W-A-T-E-R emphatically. I stood still, my whole body and attention fixed on the motions of her fingers. As the cool stream flowed over my hand, all at once, there was a strange stir within me, a misty consciousness, a sense of something remembered.

Creativity

"It was as if I had come back to life after being dead." [pp. 31-32]

CREATIVITY IN CHILDREN

Our experience of creativity in childhood shapes much of what we do in adulthood, from work to family life. The vitality— indeed, the very survival—of our society depends on nurturing adventuresome young people capable of innovative problem- solving.

Parents can encourage or suppress the creativity of their children in the home environment and by what they demand of schools. Naturally, parents want to know ways to cultivate their child's creativity—to help preserve as much of their child's wonderment and spontaneity as possible. For the child anything is possible, everything is conceivable.

But the child's natural curiosity and delight are only part of the story. The more we learn about creativity, the clearer it becomes, that it is a child's early fascination with an activity that paves the way for a creative life. This spontaneous interest leads a child to the sustained efforts and hands-on experiences that build mastery, whether at the piano, painting, or building Lego towers.

If we can avoid the narrow conception of intelligence and achievement that is traditional, there are many ways the creative spirit can be nurtured in childhood. But to do this we must begin with a basic understanding of human development.

Creativity

The reason kids don't have to be taught how to be creative is that creativity is essential for human survival. Virtually every species in the animal kingdom is born with a fully formed repertoire of reflexes and responses. Not so the human; we alone must learn and from scratch almost everything we need to know to survive.

The brain and central nervous system continue to develop and mature through childhood and into adolescence. At around eight years the skull finally knits together, encapsulating the brain. But it is not until twelve or so that the brain achieves its full adult characteristics.

From birth through childhood, the brain has many more neurons than in adulthood. On the verge of puberty, the brain undergoes a process called pruning in which millions of neurological connections die while others settle into the patterns that will be retained throughout life.

One theory holds that those neural pathways used most frequently in childhood will survive the pruning more robustly. This suggests that habits set down in childhood have a remarkable significance for the potential of the adult. It gives a profound meaning to Alexander Pope's words: "Just as the twig is bent, the tree's inclined."[pp. 58- 59]

CREATIVITY CAN'T BE FORCED

"No matter how heroic our efforts, the creative moment can't be forced; it comes to us naturally, when circumstances are right. Often, however, the demands and deadlines in our lives won't wait for the spontaneous emergence of insight. When creative energies won't flow

Creativity

on one problem or project, it helps to have another to turn to, advises University of California, psychologist Dean Simonton: "Most of history's great creators didn't just have their hands in one basket. They would have lots of different things going on. If they ran into obstacles in one area, they put it aside for a while and moved on to something else. By having multiple projects, you're more likely to have a breakthrough somewhere...you're always moving along."

Leonardo da Vinci simultaneously immersed himself in architecture, painting, city planning, science, and engineering. While doing the studies that would found the theory of evolution aboard the Beagle, Darwin also made voluminous notes on zoology, geology, and categorized facial expressions in humans and animals. Dr. Howard Gruber. psychologist at the University of Geneva who has studied Darwin's creativity, calls such far-flung interests a "network of enterprises." He suggests by shifting from project to project, creative people can bring elements and perspectives from one area that can help with another. It also means that if they've hit the stage of frustration in one project, they can put it on a mental backburner while they turn to another. [pp. 43-44]

[Goleman, Daniel; Kaufman, Paul; Ray, Michael (1992), The Creative Spirit. (pp. 18- 22, 27-32, 43-44, 58-59) New York: Penguin Group]

4 Cascading – Major brain process that takes place in the design process that enhances creativity

   4.1 Steven Kotler explains the neurochemical changes during flow states that strengthen motivation,

Creativity

creativity and learning. "The brain produces a giant cascade of neurochemistry. You get norepinephrine, dopamine, anandamide, serotonin and endorphins. All five of these are performance enhancing neurochemicals." Kotler discusses how each amplifies intellectual and cognitive performance. This is the second video in a five-part series with Steven Kotler on the "optimized brain" available in playlist form

http://bigthink.com/videos/the-neurochemistry-of-flow-states-with-steven-kotler

Simplicity

Simplicity

Simplicity is an allusive goal, very hard to achieve. When accomplished, taken for granted

1 Simplicity is extremely important. If design is done properly it evolves to simplicity

2 Multitude of layouts and iterations are necessary. It is extremely important to evolve the design to its simplest form as soon as possible so quality time is spent perfecting the right details vs. working on the details of a complex design. Simple design lends itself to precision performance.

3 When the completed design is simple, the effort that went into it is not seen. The simpler it is, the less credit is given for the effort and generally is not appreciated. Even the trained eye may miss simplicity's impact or worth, i.e. taken for granted. Unfortunately, one of the best comments one can receive is: "That's very simple. What took you so long?"

4 It's hard to make it simple

5 Einstein said, "Everything should be made as simple as possible---but no simpler."

6 Use the KISS method: Keep It Simple Stupid

7 There is beauty in simplicity – Chinese Proverb

8 "Even back then, Jobs described Apple in the terms he would use repeatedly over the years, as "an intersection between science and aesthetics." When I suggested that he seemed to be striving for an almost Zen-like simplicity in

Simplicity

his designs, he agreed, mentioning an early brochure with a single image of an apple against a white background." "Fruit, an apple," he said. "That simplicity is the ultimate sophistication. When you start looking at a problem, it seems really simple—because you don't understand its complexity. And your solutions are way too oversimplified, and they don't work. Then you get into the problem and you see it's really complicated. And you come up with all these convoluted solutions. That's where most people stop, and the solutions tend to work for a while. But the really great person will keep going and find the key underlying principle of the problem and sort of come full circle with a beautiful, elegant solution that works. And that's what we wanted to do with Mac."[The Revolution According to Steve Jobs By Steven Levy, November 29, 2011, Wired Magazine, December 2011]

9   See Appendix, DESIGN PHILOSOPHY Item 1.3 COMPLEXITY VS. TIME WITH NEW IDEAS

Master

Master

In every field, there are Masters: engineers, salesmen, athletes, musicians, scientists, actors, dancers, singers, writers, composers, investors, politicians and the list goes on. They are inspirational, a treasure, people to learn from, a joy. They are the bedrock of the field they are in.

1   The Master Traits

To become a Master one must have a love and passion for their endeavor; resulting in a relentless internal drive for perfection. One must want to do it. One must live it. One must be in tune with the natural laws. One must pay his dues. There are absolutely no shortcuts. One must want to be in it for life. It takes many years to become a Master.

There are people who could have been a Master, but for various reasons; money, prestige or a greater love for something else, they chose another path. Einstein said, "Only one who devotes himself to a cause with his whole strength and soul can be a true Master. For this reason, mastery demands all of a person."

Masters follow the Design Process striving for perfection, while creating the Building Blocks and mentoring young engineers along the way.

2   Absolutely no one started at the top of their game or profession, no one!! There are absolutely no exceptions. There were trials, tribulations, successes and failures.

In the book, Outliers, by Malcolm Gladwell, Chapter Two: The 10,000-Hour Rule, Paragraph 2, he states:

Master

"The striking thing about Ericsson's study is that he and his colleagues couldn't find any "naturals," musician's colleague floated effortlessly to the top-while practicing a fraction of the time their peers did. Nor could they find any "grinds." "Grinds," people who worked harder than everyone else, yet just didn't have what it takes to break the top ranks. Their research suggests that once a musician has enough ability to get into a top music school, the thing that distinguishes one performer from another is how hard he or she works. That's it. And what's more, the people at the very top don't work just harder or even much harder than everyone else. They work much, much harder. The idea that excellence at performing a complex task requires a critical minimum level of practice surfaces again and again in studies of expertise. In fact, researchers have settled on what they believe is the magic number for true expertise: 10,000 hours"

[Gladwell, Malcolm, (2008). Outliers. (pp. 19-20) Little Brown and Co. New York]

3   Famous Masters in other fields

Larry Bird – Legendary basketball player

Bill Belichick – NFL coach, best in history

Tom Brady – NFL quarterback, best ever

Michael Phelps – Most decorated Olympian of all time, 28 gold medals for swimming

Spielberg – Movie director

Einstein – Physicist

Master

Buffet – Investor

Hemingway – Writer

Yo-Yo Ma – Famous Cellist

Thomas Edison – Inventor

Michelangelo – Sculptor

de Goya – Artist

4 One must swallow his pride and ask questions. One must admit that he doesn't know.

5 One must dig for information

6 Must always be on the lookout for new ideas, components, new lubricants, materials or new technology

7 Must be detailed oriented

8 You must agonize over details in order to iterate toward the absolutes and perfection

9 Intuition and Feel

In design, Intuition and Feel are directly related to experience coupled with education. Do-Loops are a major factor [they are defined in Design Process chapter, Item 34]. However, Do-Loops don't always guarantee doses of reality. For instance, a young designer may call out tolerances for a locational clearance fit, on a housing bore and mating shaft. But the parts made, have looser fit than specified tolerances. Unless he measures the parts, his observations of how the parts mate and work together will result in flawed Intuition and Feel.

The designer becomes very perceptive after he has done many verified Do-Loops. As a young designer, he must calculate many things as part of the Do-Loop. In this way, he becomes in tune with the design and develops a feel. As his experience grows, he will do calculations only where needed; thereby, avoiding analysis paralysis.

In conclusion, the more you learn and do, in other words, the more Do-Loops done, the better your Intuition, Visualization and Feel are. This is extremely valuable in the design process. The formulas become built into your brain and you design with much Intuition

10 Education

Learning through education is vital. It is supplementary to Intuition and Feel as well as Mental Libraries.

The first time one must size a cantilevered beam with a load on the end. He refers to Machinery's Handbook or utilizes a software program and sees the image of the formulas shown below where, F = Force, M = Moment and V = Shear.

Master

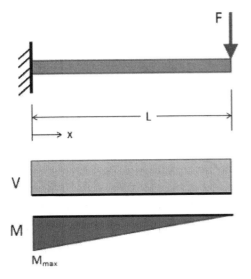

That image will remain in his brain forever and it will be remembered, that the max moment arm is at the wall and the shear is equal along the whole length. From then on, if a similar design comes up, he has a sense of where the max moment arm is, so he is already thinking he might use a short gusset near the wall and a maybe a rib along the whole length of the beam allowing for the equal shear force along the beam

Or the first time one had to heat up a part in a process, the formula is $Q = m\ c\ \Delta T$ [Q = amount of thermal energy transferred to a body; m = mass of part; c = specific heat; ΔT = final temp. − initial temp.]. Intuitively, the formula tells one the greater the temperature differential and the higher the specific heat the more thermal energy is needed. These are two factors that will help determine the size of the heating unit.

Master

10.1 These are two examples of what might be learned in school.

When one goes to college, a multitude of subjects are learned: physics, chemistry, thermal sciences and math to name a few. All these learnings come into play as a machine designer is working on a complex device.

Without the education, he will lack the depth needed and compromise a holistic approach.

There is learning in other places:

10.2 Multitude of Applications[Apps]

10.3 Many online sites. For example:

www.khanacademy

org http://www.learnengineering.org

There are many non-degreed designers who are excellent, but lack knowledge in stress analysis, heat transfer, physics, chemistry, etc. It's up to their supervisor or project engineer to provide him help in these areas, when needed.

The fact that a degreed engineer has been exposed to wide range of the sciences in school and understands the essence of them, he can design with a tremendous amount of knowledge, guiding him even before he starts his layout and calculations.

Master

11 Learning

Never stops. Every time a job is completed something new is learned. To really learn the effectiveness of one's designs he must live with them for months or years, watch them work, make improvements and always ask the question, If I was to do this job again, what would I change and what ideas would I keep. Another do-loop adding to one's intuition and feel Learn to see

12 Mental Library Directories

One must develop a wide range and extensive mental library directories. The idea is to learn the engineering basics of each component that is encountered, thereby, building another mental library directory of Building Blocks. Study and understand the engineering section of the component being used. Always be searching for new components, lubricants, materials, coatings that would solve various problems in future designs. These become Building Block directories that can be called up at any time. The more Building Blocks one has, the more creative and effective one can be.Learn the basics early and use this knowledge over and over. When you go into the Zone using key words, the Directories containing the Building Block needed can be accessed. Much like surfing the web using hypertext.

13 An example of building a mental library directory: designing a journal [shaft and housing bore] for a precise machine tool

After studying various bearing types, one has selected an 18 mm bore Timken spherical roller bearing for the precision machine tool he is designing.

Master

For the design, use the Timken catalog:
www.timken.com/pdf/10446_SRB%20Catalog.pdf
[a wealth of information]

14 How is a mental directory created?

    14.1 Study different types of bearings that would best suit the application.

    14.2 Explaine the application in detail; loads, rpm, environment it's in, lubrication, etc. to a bearing specialist to help find the right bearing

    14.3 Studying the catalog, one learns about

        14.3.1 Bearing mounting, fitting, setting and installation

        14.3.2 Shaft and housing fits

        14.3.3 Operating temperatures

        14.3.4 Bearing material limitations

        14.3.5 Lubrication

    14.4 After studying the catalog one determines the tolerance for that shaft diameter is +.0000/-0003"

        14.4.6 This is a tight tolerance. A machinist may question a young engineer, assuming he doesn't know what he's doing. The engineer states, very calmly, "I used the tolerance given in the engineering section of the

Master

catalog. This criterion was developed over many years of engineering and extensive testing in the field. I just figured they knew more about it, than you or I." [Ouch]

14.4.7 Learning the basics like mounting and lubrication, one is sensitive to making sure the design allows for the bearing to be assembled, i.e. pressed in properly, and lubricated adequately

15 Masters learn the essence of whatever they are doing.

16 Must be sensitive to surroundings and environment the design will operate in

17 It's important to know when you don't know -Aristotle

18 Knowing what question to ask is half the answer. One should never be embarrassed to ask questions

Don't be afraid to say, "I don't know." Don't be afraid to ask for help. Go to the experts for the answers whenever possible. One can find answers from other resources.

19 Four stages of learning [From Wikipedia]

unconscious – incompetence: don't know that you don't know

conscious- incompetence: know that you don't know

conscious: you know that you are competent

Master

unconscious: you are unconscious of your competence. By now, much is in-born or second nature

You are a master at stages 3&4. It becomes most difficult at stage 4 to understand how little a novice engineer knows [one forgets how little he knew at the early stages] or how little someone in a different field such as marketing, finance or management knows about design. People in other fields must take, on faith, what the masters tell them about intricacies of design; the time and effort it takes to complete complex designs. This is where 'teach and show' is important. However, it is difficult to know where to start here and if they will ever understand without 'walking in the shoes'.

Especially in stage 4, when your given a design job, because of your experience and knowledge you come up with a way to do it, relatively quickly. It is very difficult to step back and look for a better way, because of new technologies, methods, etc. Maybe there is a better way?

20 Experience

With experience one usually can grasp the difficulty of the job, whether it's possible, if it's going to be a major development or relatively straight forward with known outcomes

The experienced designer can see to the end. The designer must fight this urge: see it to the end too quickly. He should always ask himself, "Is there a better way?" "Is there new stuff out there that didn't exist previously or doesn't know about?"

Master

"In all walks of life one of the greatest obstacles to achieving presence of mind is mastery of your particular craft. It is easy to fall prey to overconfidence. On a larger scale this overconfidence can lead to something similar to Napoleon's march to Moscow. On a smaller scale you jump to conclusions fast.

This is so, because you use expert intuition in situations that call for strategic intuition. You think a situation looks familiar, but you miss the elements that make it different.

Expertise can give you a false sense of mastery. What you need instead is the Zen discipline of beginner's mind in every situation. Beginner's mind is exactly von Clausewitz's presence of mind. It does not mean that you fail to master your craft. It is a step beyond mastery, when you clear your mind of all you know, the moment you step onto the field of battle. Otherwise, you carry thoughts into the battle based the wrong Karma. You cannot fully know what forces are in play in the battle--- what moves you will need, what goal you must set---until you reach the moment of the battle itself."

[Duggan, William (2013). Strategic Intuition (p. 73) New York: Columbia University Press]

21 A Master is very adept of un-grooving his thinking [see Design Process, Item 18-19]

22 Experience should yield to youth at times

The inexperienced designer may come up with a jewel of an idea because he has a fresh creative mind and he may be more aware of a new technology that the older one is not aware of. Also, the younger engineer may not know that something is impossible and start out on a totally different track, leading to a breakthrough.

23 Pull Promotions

When a designer demonstrates time after time he is good at his job, then he becomes the clear choice for a promotion to senior designer or lead designer and he will be asked. Versus one who aggressively asks for a higher position.

The people in the department know who performs best and will take the lead from someone who has repeatedly demonstrated his ability

While at lower levels for an appropriate time the designer is building a solid foundation

24 Designer's depth of thinking

Are revealed by looking at his layouts, details and calculations. Calling out, reliefs, radii, chamfers, hardnesses, geometric tolerances, materials, finishes, etc. are a good indicator.

25 Designer's driving force

Comes from (Maslow's hierarchy)

Feeling of accomplishment

Designing and creating satisfies a basic human need

Master

Praise and appreciation

Fear of failure

Mistakes are embarrassing

The art of it

A spiritual experience

Money

26 Creative Courage

In the book, Courage to Create, by Rollo May, Chapter One, in paragraph 'Creative Courage' he describes it best.

"Whereas moral courage is the righting of wrongs, creative courage, in contrast, is the discovering of new forms, new symbols, new patterns on which a new society can be built. Every profession can and does require some creative courage. In our day, technology and engineering diplomacy, business, and certainly teaching, all of these professions and scores of others are in the midst of radical change and require courageous persons to appreciate and direct this change. The need for creative courage is in direct proportion to the degree of change the profession is undergoing. But those who present directly and immediately the new forms and symbols are the artists, the dramatists, the musicians, the painters, the dancers, the poets, and those poets of the religious sphere we call saints. They portray the new symbols, in the form of images- poetic, aural, plastic, or dramatic, as the case may be, they live out their imaginations. The symbols

Master

only dreamt about by most human beings are expressed in graphic form by the artists, but in our appreciation of the created work-let us say a Mozart quintet-we also are performing a creative act. When we engage a painting, which we have to do especially with modern art if we are authentically to see it, we are experiencing some new moment of sensibility. Some new vision is triggered in us by our contact with the painting; something unique is born in us.

This is why appreciation of the music or painting or other works of the creative person is also a creative act on our part"

[May, Rollo (1994). The Courage to Create. (pp. 21-22) New York: W. W. Norton & Co.]

27 Vision for a design

Must be fine-tuned from feedback generated from all levels

28 Mentoring

28.1 Take other designers to a higher level, which in turn takes the Master higher.

28.2 An ideal mentor

28.2.1 Would be like a coach, teaching, encouraging, building self- esteem, allowing for a mistake or two and making it fun

28.3 There are negative mentors

Master

28.3.2 I see what he does and I don't want to be like him or do it the way he does.

28.4 When the mentor talks over a design project with the engineer doing the job, many ideas will be talked about, in the effort, to set a direction. These ideas, even from a Master, must survive scaled layouts, calculations, etc. More often than not, the initial ideas will not work. Or better ideas may arise. The Master is only saying how he would start the job. It is not intended to force the initial ideas onto the final outcome. It is up to the designer to scrutinize and check out his ideas. More than likely, the Master, if doing the job, would roll out of the initial ideas, as more questions are asked, layouts and calculations are performed.

29 Conceit and brilliance can mask unknowns.

When bright people are wrong you have a problem. They usually have good logical reasons why they are wrong. Don't let brilliance get in the way. Sometimes brilliance stems from people who have great minds that are exceptional at assimilating facts and figures, deriving formulas, theories, then blindly following them and not receptive to simpler ways. Be careful that brilliance doesn't obscure the true reality of the problem and solutions. Ideas of what is needed must be influenced by people who are attuned to the environment it will be used in, their noses in it and living it.

30 Admit mistakes.

Master

Admitting mistakes has a way of clearing the air. It makes you strive to be error free, because it is always embarrassing to admit mistakes. If you make too many mistakes then you are not a Master, maybe even poor at your job.

One bares his soul and identifies with his work and must take the criticism that goes along with it. This makes one a better designer: you make sure your work is good and based on sound principles to minimize mistakes.

31 Standing on the Shoulders

We stand on the shoulders of the Masters and our mentors, they will be with us forever. Like the work of many masters who have lived throughout the ages, masters of music, art, science, philosophy and spiritual masters. Mankind has stood on their shoulders, as in some way, the people who follow us will stand on our shoulders. We can learn from each other.

There will always be other masters. Why are they so far and few between? Because only a small minority will push for perfection, have the curiosity, always search for the higher logic and always ask why. Many things get in the way: balance, job promotions, not dedicated to the pain and hard thinking that goes with it or they don't love it. The masters are not afraid to think. Thinking is very hard work and can be very exhausting. Coming up with new ideas takes a degree of risk taking

32 Visionaries

Master

Visionaries have the vision, The Masters make the vision happen. The visionary, in his own mind, thinks it can be done and has confidence it can be done.

Masters follow the Design Process while in the Zone with a focused effort, striving for perfection and Simplicity. The end result is a design that ultimately brings profit to the Company to keep the process going.

33 Always be willing to yield to a higher logic

In the book, Courage to Create, by Rollo May, Chapter One, in paragraph 5, One Paradox of Courage, he says:

"A curious paradox characteristic of every kind of courage here confronts us. It is the seeming contradiction that we must be fully committed, but we must also be aware, at the same time, that we might possibly be wrong. This dialectic relationship between conviction and doubt is characteristic of the highest types of courage, and give the lie to the simplistic definitions that identify courage with mere growth. People who claim to be absolutely convinced that their stand is the only right one are dangerous. Such conviction is the essence not only of dogmatism, but of its more destructive cousin, fanaticism. It blocks off the user from learning new truth, and it is a dead giveaway of unconscious doubt. The person then has to double his or her protest in order to quiet not only the opposition but his or her own unconscious doubts as well......It is infinitely safer to know that the man at the top has his doubt, as you and I have ours, yet has the courage to move ahead in spite of these doubts. In contrast to the fanatic who has stockaded himself against new truth, the person with the courage to believe and at the same time to admit

Master

his doubts is flexible and open to new learning......The relationship between commitment and doubt is by no means an antagonistic one. Commitment is healthiest when it is not without doubt, but in spite of doubt. To believe fully and at the same moment to have doubts is not at all a contradiction: it presupposes a greater respect for truth, an awareness that truth always goes beyond anything that can be said or done at any given moment. To every thesis there is an antithesis, and to this is a synthesis. Truth is a never-dying process."

[May, Rollo (1994). The Courage to Create. (pp. 20-21) New York: W. W. Norton & Co.]

Stated another way

"Buddha Thought: We must not be attached to a view or a doctrine, even a Buddhist one.

.... The Buddha said that if in a certain moment or place you adopt something as the absolute truth, and you attach to that, then you will no longer have any chance to reach the truth. Even when the truth comes and knocks on your door, and asks you to open the door, you won't recognize it. So you must not be too attached to dogma--to what you believe, and to what you perceive."

[in an interview with Diane Wolkstein featured in Parabola Vol 30 No 4]

"To reach your goal, you give up your goal, to achieve your desire you suspend desire. You open your mind in order to let the best possible actions from the past combine to reach the best possible goal in the future"

Master

[Duggan, William (2013). Strategic Intuition (p. 75) New York: Columbia University Press]

34 Question All the Answers

As stated before, one must question all the answers all the time. In this way, the truths will be revealed while the untruths will yield. The analogy: kernels of the wheat remain while the chaff is blown away. One must deepen his understanding of all things gradually widening his scope, eventually becoming more in tune with reality.

35 Give credit to whomever comes up with the ideas, always

36 One must always remember the 'Golden Rule'

37 To become a Master always, without fail, strive for perfection

Management

Management

Management can affect all The Elements of Design. They can nurture Creativity or not, they can nurture or hire Masters or not, they can create an environment that allows people to work in the Zone creating the Building Blocks or not. They can demand Simplicity or not. [See Appendix, Management]

1   Management should match engineering projects with in-house capability

2   When there are too many projects or lack of expertise, outside sources should be considered

3   If a design and build house is to be used, there are some requirements and questions that should be considered. Although these requirements are geared to automatic assembly equipment, they apply to other types of projects as well

    3.1   Been in business 10+ years designing and building the type of equipment or devices you need

    3.2   Is design and build their only business

    3.3   What type of CAD software is used

    3.4   Annual sales

    3.5   Are all their employees permanent [not a job shop]

    3.6   Can provide full documentation, in a usable form that can be duplicated and revised. The documentation of the designed equipment should include mechanical, electrical and pneumatic

Management

drawings along with operation and maintenance manuals.

3.6.1 They will resist this and tell you it will cost more

3.6.2 The mantra: The documentation should be complete enough to duplicate the equipment or system by another company, because, they might not be there when you need to make a duplicate or too costly. You don't want to be beholden to them. The documentation can be revised for improvements and changes

3.6.3 They may use some of their proprietary designs, therefore will not provide documentation. This must be negotiated

3.7 Provide company personnel info: time with company, experience in the field, education and titles

3.7.4 Engineers, technicians, machinist, clerical, administrators

3.8 Machine shop facilities list

3.8.5 Have quality control capabilities

3.9 Floor Space: office, Machine shop, assembly area

3.10 Utilize program management systems: Gantt Charts, etc.

Management

3.11 Provide references from companies who have had similar recent projects completed

3.12 Dun & Bradstreet [or equivalent] check. Check with Better Business Bureau

3.13 After a house meets all the criteria and all things being equal, pick the one closest to you, preferably one that can be visited in one day

    3.13.6 Currently with all the new technology, this is not as important as it used to be, but, it is still best to visit, touch and feel the equipment and develop a rapport with the ones directly involved with the project

Tidbits

Tidbits

Tidbits can be comingled with The Elements of Design

1 Machine Designer's Kit

Scientific calculator
Screw Calculator from Holo-Chrome
Reality Stick (ruler taped to your CAD screen)
Drill sizes (including tap drills) & decimal equivalents
Machinery's Handbook
Mark's Handbook
Swiss Army Knife – Victroinox Super Tinker

Blades are hardened to 55 Rc. Can perform a scratch test on a piece of metal to determine if it's been hardened. Carry it with you, always. When flying, if you can't put it in checked luggage, leave it home. I've given two away at the airport, because I forgot to

2 Scan trade magazines and journals for commercial items, technical information and new technology. Build a library of catalogs [links to them]

3 CAD Systems

CAD is a great tool, but the creativity, attention to detail and the drive for perfection lay within your mind

Tidbits

4   Estimations: Time and Money

If you haven't done a similar job, double your time and money estimates. This SWAG (Some-Wild-Ass-Guess) takes into consideration that there will always be many things missed, that really can't be known until one gets into the job. New information that arrives while designing may change the course of the design, adding more time and money than originally thought.

If you have done something very similar, add 10-15%

5   Getting it right the first time

I didn't have time to do it right, so I had to do it over again
Minimizes scrap, meetings and redoing the device

6   The builders and doers

One should have a tremendous respect and empathy for people who build, fabricate and design the stuff. It's where the rubber meets the road. It's very visible and bullshit doesn't work. It's where the mistakes are usually very obvious.

7   Design Characteristics

The design must look good and professionally done. User will treat it with respect and make it work.

Tidbits

8 Always state source of information gathered

9 Always date catalogs, memos, notes, your work

10   When talking to suppliers or people you need information from, have a list of all the questions that need to be answered in front of you and check them off as they are answered. Invariably, you will go off on tangents. The list will ensure all questions are answered

11 I never met anyone who did not want to do a good job

12 Save the layouts, one may come back to use a portion of earlier ideas

13 If a numbering system must be developed, do not attach any significance to the number other than chronological If the number has some significance, there will always be an exception

14 Forecasting the future

"There is an important distinction betweenforecasting the future and determining probability for a particular event, but the relationship between probabilities and forecasting is often misunderstood. As a simple illustration imagine a set of seven assumptions leading to a single conclusion. Each assumption has a 90% chance

Tidbits

of being right. Intuitively we think that with such high probability for each assumption we'd enjoy a very good chance our conclusion's being correct. In fact, the odds are less than fifty-fifty (.9 x .9 x .9 x .9 x .9 x .9 x .9 = 47.8 %)

> Psychologist Daniel Kahneman and Amos Tversky, in their research on decision-making, find that people consistently overestimate the probability of future scenarios that are constructed from a series of individually probable events." [*The Renewal Factor,* by Robert H. Waterman, Jr. page 35]

Epilogue

Epilogue

Below are subjects that are integral parts of The Elements of Design

1   Nature's Way of Design

    1.1   Nature achieves its goals (whatever they are) by doing many, many iterations (evolution or billions and billions of do-loops). Nature's do- loops are taking place with seemingly no intelligence under a system we do not understand

2   Vision's Place

    2.1   The president must have the vision of what he wants his company to be, where he wants it to go, what needs to be done and how things are to be done. Leave the details to the people doing the work. "Authority should go with knowledge and experience that is where obedience is due, no matter whether it is up the line or down" (Mary Parker Follett). That vision must be fine-tuned from feedback generated from all levels

3   Details

    3.1   Details can be all consuming. The answers are in the details. Details guide and fine tune the vision.

    3.2   Extremely important. If wrong, details can kill the design. Every tolerance, chamfer, radius, hardness, coating, etc. are important. Details have the inherent ability to change the course of the design. Get it right the first time to avoid the infamous statement:

Epilogue

"I didn't have time to do it right so I had to do it over again."

4   Third Generation Design

4.1   It isn't until the third generation before the design is mature (general rule of thumb)

5   Teams

5.1   Hierarchy must be minimized

5.1.1   It's like the brain telling the fingers and feet how to play the piano; put one or two people between the brain and the fingers and the music would not have the right tempo or emphasis and the sound would be chaotic. Without a symphony orchestra conductor, the music would not sound right.

5.2   All disciplines are important.

Marketing ensures that you are designing and building the right thing with all the right features. Designing is creating the right device at a targeted cost. Manufacturing is building the right thing to the specifications. There should be continual interaction between these three disciplines. The design specification must be frozen before designing starts. Without good marketing, one could have the best engineers designing the best device in the world that no one wants!

6   Quantum leaps of knowledge

Epilogue

6.1 Happens when an experienced engineer joins a company. When working with outside firms, the same is true. There is a wealth of talent and knowledge to be tapped.

Downsizing a department or fast growth forces a company to go outside, thereby, enhancing this phenomenon. Cross-functional teams bring diverse knowledge to work on a project. Critical functions must always stay inside with the eye to get help from the outside

7 Teach and Show

7.1 Use facts and numbers not emotions. If people understand then they won't resist so much

8 Balance

8.1 One must balance his life. It's hard to do in the zone. One must learn to enter the zone and exit it. If one is in the zone too long, family, friends, and your balance suffer. After one exits the zone, the subconscious is working. Sometimes, when you're relaxing or spending quality time with the family, a great idea pops into your head, an idea that may not have germinated if you were still in the zone wrapped up in details. Family and friends are extremely important. It's like you are on a large, heavy (high-inertia) disk, supported in the middle by a pointed column. The disk has three segments. One is work, another is play, and the third is quietude. If you stay in one segment, the disk starts to tip in that direction. If you go too far out or stay too long on

Epilogue

any segment, it will start to tip, so much so that you may slide off or the disk may come off its supporting column. One can find an optimum amount of time in each segment so as to never slide off. But sometimes you must unbalance your life to meet a goal. If you do it too often, you and your family will suffer immeasurably. Life is a balancing act. It's hard to do it right.

9   "While he's a high achiever, Michael Hendrix [of IDEO] isn't a workaholic. "I'm more relaxed. IDEO is more relaxed. Of course, you have those moments when you have the idea and you don't want to stop working and so you stay all night. But as a culture, we encourage people to eat well, get lots of rest, stay happy. Because as a creative person that's when your best work happens. The tortured artist coming up with a great idea is actually a great myth."

[Boston Sunday Globe 27-December-2015 Business Page G2]

10 "Hendrix's dream job would be working with NASA on the design of a spaceship to take people to Mars. He believes such a ship ought to be beautiful, as well as functional. The more highly technical something is, the more beautiful it can be. Apple figured that out. Beauty has inherent value. For the people who are on that journey, we need to design for their own peace of mind, for their own confidence. All that really matters."

[Boston Sunday Globe 27-December-2015 Business Page G2]

11 We learn to see

Epilogue

12 Tip of the iceberg

Any design is just the tip of the iceberg analogy. Each master, each person, will add to the immense collective knowledge within the universe, infinitesimal as it might be. When the designer starts to work, he is immediately in touch with the results of millions, maybe billions, of man hours of work in the calculator, the books, the CAD system, the commercial components, metallurgy, lubrication, materials, and even the building he is in, to name only a few things. We are truly standing on the shoulders of people who have been before us. As Robert Kennedy said, "Each time a man stands up for an ideal, or acts to improve the lot of others, or strikes out against injustice, he sends forth a tiny ripple of hope, and crossing each other from a million different centers of energy and daring, those ripples build a current which can sweep down the mightiest wall of oppression and resistance." To paraphrase the statement in a machine design sense, each time a man designs or builds something to improve the lot of others or strikes out to improve something, he sends forth a tiny ripple, and crossing each other from a million different centers of energy and daring, those ripples build a current that can make sweeping changes to mankind. Examples include the wheel, electricity, transistor, radio and TV, computers, the internet, the airplane, ball bearings, metallurgy, lubrication, on and on. There is a tremendous intelligence already incorporated in the designs that we all take for granted. The present designer's value added is indeed extremely small compared to the work done through the ages. Frankly, it's quite humbling. It is almost ludicrous to say, "See what I've done."

13 Truth=Reality

Epilogue

13.1 Minimizing the ego and being humble, allows one to be more in tune with his surroundings, more perceptive and setting the mind in a state to be receptive to new learnings

13.2 Your reality is what you perceive it to be. One must always strive to evolve it to a truer reality. This is an ongoing process that is difficult at best

13.3 Live the truth and become it. You will finally become what you think and what you strive for

14 Strive for perfection, settle for excellence

Quotes

Quotes

These are quotes that relate to The Elements of Design. Some have been used in the other chapters to make a related point

1. Strive for perfection, settle for excellence
   - Don Hadfield

2. It's hard to make it simple – Don Hadfield

3. Simple design lends itself to precision performance
   - Don Hadfield

4. Gentlemen, we are going to relentlessly chase perfection, knowing full well we will not catch it, because nothing is perfect. But we are going to relentlessly chase it, because in the process we will catch excellence. -Vince Lombardi

5. There is beauty in simplicity – Chinese Proverb [found in a fortune cookie]

6. The formulation of a problem is often more essential than its solution – Einstein

7. Only one who devotes himself to a cause with his whole strength and soul can be a true master – Einstein

8. It's important to know when you don't know – Aristotle

9. Authority should go with knowledge and experience, that is where obedience is due, no matter whether it is up the line or down – Mary Parker Follett

10. When Health is absent, Wisdom cannot reveal itself, Art cannot become manifest, Strength cannot be exerted, Wealth is useless and Reason is powerless
    – Herophiles 300 BC.

Quotes

11. Oh, when you were young, did you question all the answers -Wasted on the Way-Crosby, Stills & Nash

12. 1% inspiration 99% perspiration
    – Thomas Edison

13. The moment one commits, Providence acts, too – Goethe

14. Talent develops in quiet places, character in the full current of human life. – Goethe

15. Don't be blinded by brilliance – Don Hadfield

16. Smart people do dumb things
    – Charlie Munger

17. Man's character is his fate – Heraclitus

18. What can be measured can be improved
    – Bill Gates

19. Perfection is subjective rather than absolute
    – Don Hadfield

20. "Don't let perfect be the enemy of good."
    "It's derived from a similar phrase in the writing of Voltaire and it's a sentiment I always felt had real relevance when I was in the business world... about the need to keep the wheels of commerce turning rather than being concerned with getting everything absolutely right." – Tips To Help Tame Perfectionism by Victor Lipman, Forbes Magazine, MAR 13, 2014

Quotes

21. A foolish consistency is the hobgoblin of little minds
    – Ralph Waldo Emerson

22. There's never time to do it right, but there's always time to do it over – Jack Bergman

23. It's unwise to pay too much, but it's worse to pay too little. When you pay too much, you lose a little money. When you pay too little, you sometimes lose everything – John Ruskin

24. It's a bad plan that allows no modification
    – Publilius Syrus

25. The path of wisdom invites us to walk with a humble heart – Terry Tempest Williams

26. Whether you think you can or think you can't, you're right
    – Henry Ford

27. Making the simple complicated is common place; making the complicated simple, awesomely simple, that's creativity
    – Charles Mingus

28. If you never change your mind, why have one? – Edward de Bono

29. It is not the strongest of the species that survive, nor the most intelligent, but the most responsive to change – Charles Darwin

Quotes

30. Luck is the residue of good design
    – John Milton

31. No problem can withstand the assault of sustained thinking – Voltaire

32. Do not quench your inspiration and your imagination; do not become the slave of your model – Vincent Van Gogh

33. Teach the tongue to say, "I do not know."
    – Maimonides

34. The best way to predict the future is to invent it
    – Alan Kay

35. The lack of focus can result in disaster
    – Chuck Yeager

36. You create reality with your intentions
    – Gary Zukav author of The Seat of the Soul

37. There are three classes of people, those who see, those who see when they are shown, those who don't see.
    – Leonardo daVinci

38. Exhilaration is that feeling you get just after a great idea hits you, and just before you realize what's wrong with it – Rex Harrison

39. If you wish to make a man your enemy, tell him simply, 'You are wrong.' This method works every time
    – Henry C Link

Quotes

40. In matters of principle, stand like a rock, in matters of taste, swim with the current
    – Thomas Jefferson

41. The man who insists upon seeing with perfect clearness before he decides, never decides
    – Henri Fredric Amiel

42. People forget how fast you did a job, but, they remember how well you did it
    – Howard Newton

43. The older I get, the more amazed I am

Note:

The Don Hadfield quotes, I thought, were originals by me. As one ponders certain things, thoughts come to your mind and they become a quote that you use. More often than not, others have uttered the same quote.

When you're dealing with a truth, it has been there forever and people, in all walks of life, just discover them.

Philosophy

Philosophy

1. Happiness

    Happiness is the greatest paradox in nature. It can grow in any soil, live in any conditions. It defies environment. It comes from within; it is the revelation of the depths of the inner life as light and Heat proclaim the sun from which they radiate. Happiness consists not of having, but of being; Not of possessing, but of enjoying. A martyr at the stake may have happiness that a king on his throne might envy. Man is the creator of his own happiness; it is The aroma of a life lived in harmony with high ideals for what a man has, he may be dependent on others, what he is, rests with him alone. Happiness is the soul's joy in the possession of the intangible. It is the warm glow of a heart at peace with itself.
    – William George Jordan

2. Truth

    Our world is torn apart by differing creeds, doctrines, mantras, misconceptions, such as: "We are the chosen ones". Untruths are perpetrated by many well-meaning religious leaders, teachers and parents, reinforced by inspired religious writings mistaken as the truth. When taught by people one trusts they are embraced as the truth and become unyielding to the new-found truths. Whether realized or not, we are all created via the same way from the same source. There are no chosen ones. There are many good ways and teachings in virtually all religions, the best being the 'Golden Rule': "Treat others as you would like to be treated." As the truth is slowly revealed the ism's the ist's will fade and the world will become closer and become as one.

Philosophy

Whether an atheist or a religious zealot, all appreciate a beautiful sunrise or sunset, a snow-capped mountain range, the vivid colors of an autumn landscape, the sound of a babbling crystal clear brook, the beautiful color and fragrance of a flower, the blue expanse of the ocean, a beautiful moon-lit night, a vivid rainbow, the brilliant stars on a cold clear night. These are all moments of sensing the creation. We all cherish friendships; we all fall in love. It makes no difference what one's religious beliefs, we all appreciate the same things. This is the creation we are all a part of. While the truth is being reveled, the power of love and kindness, along with the beauty of the creation will be there. Do lots of small acts of kindness. Practice patience, giving others time to learn the truth. Be humble so you can gracefully yield your misconceptions to that of the truth. Reflect on who you are and what you are learning. Question all the 'answers'. Balance your life so no one thing takes you over. Paraphrasing one of our greatest spiritual leaders: "Learn the Truth. The Truth will set you free."
– Don Hadfield

3. A Successful Man

    Looks forward to each day as a new opportunity;
    Knows his goals and sets his own course in life;
    Is sensitive to the thoughts of others; Graciously values opinions, respects truth, And gives praise;
    Finds enjoyment in lending a hand, And sees possibilities in challenges;
    Is most grateful for the respect of family and friends;
    Takes pride in himself, Toned in body and character; Has faith

Philosophy

And has confidence in himself.
– Elizabeth Lucas

4. Success

To laugh often and much,
To win the respect of intelligent people And affection of children
To earn the appreciation of honest critics And endue the betrayal of false friends To appreciate beauty
To find the best in others,
To leave the world a little bit better, Whether by a healthy child,
A garden patch or a redeemed social condition;
To know even one life has breathed easier Because you have lived,
This is to have succeeded
– Ralph Waldo Emerson

5. Death of a Company Culture

My first days at Hewlett Packard [HP] 1993 were involved in Orientation Sessions where they talked about the 'HP Way', use of their products, ethics, etc. I completely bought into it. I worked on a team that was very intelligent, with great leaders. The goal was developing leading edge products. The team worked very well together with the same mind set, doing it the 'HP Way'. The feeling was that HP cared about their employees. They prided themselves in hiring only the best and their salary structure was among the highest. If economic times were tough, they might cut salaries to save jobs and restore the pay when things got better; thereby, keeping the talent in place.

Philosophy

Everyone respected one another and cherished each one's special talents. If you saw a project you might like to work on, they certainly would consider it. Virtually everyone would go the extra mile to make projects successful. There were stories of the past, one being: Bill Hewlett, going out on the factory floor, asking some of the employees what they were working on, showing a genuine interest in their comments.

The 'HP Way' culture changed rather abruptly when A few of the key Health Care Division leaders left and Carly Fiorina became president. This was the first time HP went outside for their top executive. Her career was based on marketing, most likely, a person who had never designed and built anything. A person who didn't understand the power of the 'HP Way' and making a statement 'Perfect enough'. With all these changes, the whole culture changed. HP split up and became Agilent. The President of Agilent, who was brought up with the 'HP Way', quickly became more interested in the bottom line. In his first site meeting with us, he said, "If Agilent didn't meet their numbers the analysts would kill us." It became obvious that he was more interested in his stock options than anything else. They hired a vice president who became second man in charge. He was the former President of Packard Bell which had previously filed for bankruptcy. In his first appearance at our site, he stated that we needed to go to the 'Top of the Mountain' and grow 30% per year. That was very disheartening, revealing he had no concept of our business model or the products we made. It seemed that the new executives were managers, not leaders, that had no experience of designing and building things and expertise was not appreciated as it had been in the past. Agilent started to work on sending most of the Healthcare

Philosophy

Division's operations to Singapore. Phillips bought out those divisions and squelched the Singapore idea. The 'HP Way' culture had died.
– Don Hadfield

6. Forever Young by Bob Dylan
    May God's bless and keep you always
    May your wishes all come true
    May you always do for others
    And let others do for you
    May you build a ladder to the stars
    And climb on every rung
    May you stay forever young
    Forever young forever young
    May you stay forever young
    May you grow up to be righteous
    May you grow up to be true
    May you always know the truth
    And see the lights surrounding you
    May you always be courageous
    Stand upright and be strong
    May you stay forever young
    Forever young forever young
    May you stay forever young
    May your hands always be busy
    May your feet always be swift
    May you have a strong foundation
    When the winds of changes shift
    May your heart always be joyful
    And may your song always be sung
    May you stay forever young
    Forever young forever young
    May you stay forever young
    – Bob Dylan – Songwriter

Philosophy

7. "Give us grace and strength to forbear and to persevere. Give us courage and gaiety, and the quiet mind. Spare to us our friends, soften to us our enemies. Bless us, if it may be, in all our innocent endeavors. If it may not, give us the strength to encounter that which is to come, that we may be brave in peril, constant in tribulation, temperate in wrath, and in all changes of fortune, and down to the gates of death, loyal and loving to one another."
   – Robert Louis Stevenson

8. As every past generation has had to disenthrall itself from an inheritance of truisms and stereotypes, so in our own time we must move on from the reassuring repetition of stale phrases to a new, difficult, but essential confrontation with reality. For the great enemy of the truth is very often not the lie—deliberate, contrived, and dishonest— but the myth—persistent, persuasive, and unrealistic. Too often we hold fast to the clichés of our forebears. We subject all facts to a prefabricated set of interpretations. We enjoy the comfort of opinion without the discomfort of thought.
   – John F. Kennedy – Yale University Commencement Speech June 1962

9. Look to this day
   For it is life, the very life of life
   For yesterday is already a dream,
   And tomorrow is only a vision
   But today, well lived, makes every yesterday
   A dream of happiness and every tomorrow a vision of hope
   – From the Sanskrit

10. Nothing real can be threatened it should be easy to defend and support
    – Tarah Sinh – Spiritual Leader

A Little Bit of Humor

A Little Bit of Humor

The Knack:

A funny cartoon by Dilbert – The Knack At YouTube, in the search box type: Dilbert The Knack

Ain't it the Truth

An Engineer is a man who knows a great deal about very little and who goes along learning more and more about less and less until finally he knows practically everything about nothing

A Salesman, on the other hand, is a man who knows very little about many things and keeps learning less and less about more and more, until he knows practically nothing about everything

A Purchasing Agent starts out knowing everything about everything, but ends up Knowing nothing about anything, due to his association with Engineers and Salesmen [Author unknown]

The Flea Joke [false conclusions]

A professor was given a government grant to study fleas. He picked off a flea from Spot, his cocker spaniel, and took it to the lab. He placed the flea on his work bench and said, "Fly flea." and the flea took off. He repeated the experiment five times and it flew took off without fail. For the next experiment, he ripped off its wings, placed it back on the bench and said, "Fly flea", but, it just meandered around. Again, he barked the command, "Fly flee" but nothing happened. Then the professor yelled, **"FLY FLEA, FLY FLEE, FLY FLEE"** but the

A Little Bit of Humor

flee just meandered. In the conclusion of his report, he wrote, "When one rips off the wings of a flea, it becomes deaf." [Author unknown]

Better Writing for Engineering Reports

As the mechanical engineering lab professor was returning the graded reports of the last lab assignment, he said: "You students did a good job on the experiment, but your writing skills need to improve. When you get out in industry, you will have to write reports and it's important to use good English. You might look to the Bible for some good examples." The next lab assignment was to determine the efficiency of a steam turbine. One of the students, wrote for the conclusion in his report: "And it came to pass, that the efficiency of the steam turbine was 110% and Jesus wept. [Author unknown]

A Little Bit of Humor

Non Sequitur by Wiley

"In the cafeteria just after lunch; well, not just after more like during lunch, about 12:30, say 12:30; give or take a few minutes, I leaned back in my chair. It was one of those aluminum chairs, good strength to weight, not like titanium but then titanium would be a bit of an overkill. Anyway, I overheard one of the girls talking about how boring she thought engineers could be."

A Little Bit of Humor

Appendix

MACHINE   DESIGN

AND

RELATED   SUBJECTS

BY: DON A. HADFIELD
      FEB 1987
      REVISED DEC 1990

OUTLINE

DESIGN PHILOSOPHY

1. SIMPLICITY

2. TECHNOLOGIES & TECHNIQUES TO BE LEARNED

3. CONCENTRATED EFFORT

4. MACHINE PERFORMANCE VS LEARNING CURVE

5. EVOLUTION OF A MACHINE

6. MACHINE DESIGN PROCESS

7. COMMON THEMES OF MACHINES

8. CREATIVITY

9. ENGINEERS CHARACTER

10. OUTSIDE ENGINEERING

11. OUTSIDE MACHINE SHOPS

12. DESIGN MANAGEMENT

13. FINE ART OF ENGINEERING

14. QUOTES

MANAGEMENT

1. QUICK FIXES, CRISIS MANAGEMENT

2. SHORT TERM VS LONG TERM

3. DEVELOPING HUMAN RESOURCES

4. VISION

5. SURVIVAL

6. HIGH TECH RISKS

7. GENERAL COMMENTS

DESIGN PHILOSOPHY

BASIC TRUTHS OF IN-PLANT MACHINE DESIGN

THROUGH THE YEARS OF MY EXPERIENCE, IT HAS BECOME VERY CLEAR THAT
THERE ARE CERTAIN BASIC TRUTHS FOR IN-PLANT MACHINE DESIGN. THESE
TRUTHS ARE ALMOST ALWAYS SELF EVIDENT AND CAN BE APPLIED TO MANY OTHER
DISCIPLINES. MOST TRUTHS ARE REINFORCED BY COMMON SENSE, ALTHOUGH, IN
A WORLD OF RAPID CHANGE AND BOTTOM LINE PRESSURES, THESE TRUTHS BECOME
UNCLEAR, THEREFORE, ARE NOT ALWAYS REINFORCED.

1. IT'S HARD TO MAKE IT SIMPLE.

    1.1 IT TAKES CONCENTRATED EFFORT, CONTINUITY OF PERSONNEL,
        CREATIVITY, INTELLIGENCE AND A STRIVING FOR EXCELLENCE.

    1.2 ANYONE CAN MAKE SOMETHING COMPLICATED.

    1.3 COMPLEXITY VS. TIME WITH NEW IDEAS.

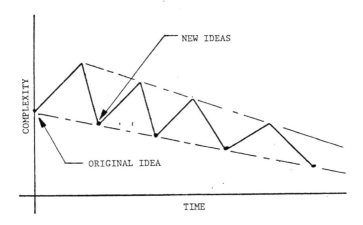

    1.4 GOOD SIMPLE DESIGN EVOLVES.

2. IN EVERY INDUSTRY, THERE ARE MANY TECHNOLOGIES AND TECHNIQUES
THAT ARE USED. SOME OF THESE ARE PECULIAR TO THAT THAT INDUSTRY.
THESE TECHNOLOGIES MUST BE LEARNED BY INSIDE PEOPLE.

    2.1 SOME OF THESE TECHNOLOGIES THAT MUST BE MASTERED AT THE
        CIRCUIT PROTECTION DIVISION ARE: FILLING, TINNING, TESTING,
        CRIMPING, MACHINING, SOLDERING, ASSEMBLY, FLUXING, STAMPING,
        DRILLING, PINNING, SLITTING, PLATING, PULTRUSION, AUTOMATION
        TECHNOLOGIES.

    2.2 ALL THESE TECHNOLOGIES MUST BE INCORPORATED BY ENGINEERING
        THEM INTO PLANT EQUIPMENT.

2.2.1   TECHNOLOGIES AND MACHINES THAT HAVE ALREADY BEEN
        MASTERED IN INDUSTRY SHOULD BE PURCHASED.
        (DON'T REINVENT THE WHEEL)

        2.2.1.1   WHENEVER POSSIBLE BUYING STANDARD
                  EQUIPMENT IS THE BEST CHOICE. IT HAS
                  BEEN DEBUGGED, PROVEN IN THE FIELD, AND
                  IS CHEAPER BECAUSE UNITS HAVE BEEN MADE
                  IN QUANTITY WITH ENGINEERING COSTS
                  DEFRAYED.

        2.2.1.2   IF THE MACHINE OR DEVICE CAN'T BE
                  PURCHASED, THE MECHANICAL DESIGN GROUP
                  OR AN OUTSIDE DESIGN HOUSE WOULD DO THE
                  JOB (SEE ITEM 10).

2.2.2   TECHNOLOGIES AND MACHINES PECULIAR TO FUSE
        BUILDING THAT HAVE NOT BEEN MASTERED ON THE
        OUTSIDE WORLD MUST BE DEVELOPED BY INSIDE PEOPLE
        OR BY WORKING VERY CLOSELY WITH OUTSIDE PEOPLE.

2.2.3   MOST OF THE TIME, ONE HAS TO LEARN HOW TO DO IT
        RIGHT ONLY ONCE; FROM THAT POINT ON, YOUR
        CHANCES FOR SUCCESS ARE GREATLY ENHANCED. ONCE
        THE TECHNOLOGY IS LEARNED, IT MAY BE APPLIED OVER
        AND OVER AGAIN WITH HIGH SUCCESS.

2.2.4   THE TECHNOLOGIES MUST BE RECORDED IN THE FORM OF
        DETAILED MECHANICAL, PNEUMATIC AND ELECTRICAL
        DRAWINGS AS WELL AS DETAILED PROCESS
        DOCUMENTATION. ONLY IN THIS WAY CAN THINGS BE
        REPEATED, ESPECIALLY IF KEY PEOPLE LEAVE.

3. TO ACHIEVE SUCCESS IN MACHINE DESIGN, THERE MUST BE
    A CONCENTRATED EFFORT ALONG WITH QUALITY TIME.

    3.1 CREATIVITY CANNOT BE ACHIEVED WITH CONSTANT INTERRUPTION
         AND UNREASONABLE DEMANDS.

4. MACHINE PERFORMANCE VS. LEARNING CURVE.

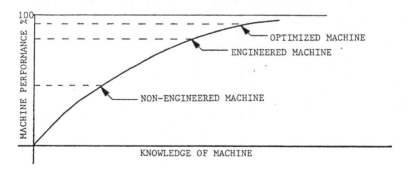

5. IN THE EVOLUTION OF THE DESIGN FOR A MACHINE, OPTIMIZATION DOESN'T USUALLY OCCUR UNTIL THE THIRD GENERATION; AND ONLY IF, THERE ARE QUALITY PEOPLE ON THE JOB WHO HAVE BEEN PRESENT FOR ALL THREE GENERATIONS.

6. THE MACHINE DESIGN PROCESS IS ANALOGOUS TO A SERVO GUIDANCE SYSTEM

   6.1 AT THE BEGINNING, A MACHINE DESIGNER IS GIVEN INPUT (INFORMATION) WHICH SETS HIM ON A COURSE. AS THE TASK PROCEEDS, HE MUST DIG FOR INFORMATION FROM WITHIN THE PLANT AND MUST DO SOME BASIC RESEARCH, WHICH BECOMES NEW INPUT (INFORMATION AND KNOWLEDGE) TO GUIDE HIM THROUGH THE DESIGN. THIS INPUT USUALLY FORCES MANY CORRECTIONS IN COURSE. IN FACT, THEY MAY CONTRADICT THE INPUTS GIVEN AT THE BEGINNING. IN THE END, MORE OFTEN THAN NOT, THE MACHINE IS QUITE DIFFERENT THAN ORIGINAL CONCEPTS. IE: THE COURSE CHANGED MANY TIMES IN THE PROCESS OF DESIGNING THE MACHINE.

7. COMMON THEME OF MACHINES.

   7.1 MAXIMUM USE OF COMMERCIAL PARTS AND PROVEN TECHNOLOGY.

   7.2 DESIGN MACHINES FOR FAMILIES OF FUSES.

      7.2.1 EASE OF CONVERSION FROM ONE SIZE TO ANOTHER.

      7.2.2 FLEXIBILITY.

   7.3 GOOD DOCUMENTATION.

      7.3.1 FOR DUPLICATION.

      7.3.2 FOR ENHANCEMENTS.

      7.3.3 FOR REPLACEMENT OF WORN PARTS.

      7.3.4 CONTINUITY.

   7.4 MODULAR CONSTRUCTION (SEE ARTICLES).

      7.4.1 ALLOWS COMPLEX MACHINES OR SUBASSEMBLIES TO BE SUBDIVIDED.

         7.4.1.1 ONE DESIGNER CAN BE ASSIGNED TO EACH MODULE PERMITTING MULTIPLE PEOPLE WORKING SIMULTANEOUSLY ON MACHINE AND EACH ONE HAVING NEARLY FULL CONTROL WITH A CONCENTRATED EFFORT ON HIS MODULE.

         7.4.1.2 EACH MODULE CAN BE DEVELOPED AND PERFECTED OFF-LINE.

7.4.1.3   EACH MODULE COULD BE DESIGNED IN-HOUSE OR
           OUTSIDE, FABRICATED IN OUR TOOL ROOM OR
           AT OUTSIDE SHOPS.

7.4.1.4   A MODULE COULD BE INCORPORATED IN AN
           AUTOMATIC ASSEMBLY MACHINE, A CAROUSEL
           ASSEMBLY SYSTEM OR AS A STAND ALONE
           DEVICE FOR A HAND ASSEMBLY OPERATION.

7.4.1.5   ALLOWS LARGE JOBS TO BE SPLIT UP AND DONE
           BY DESIGNERS OR FABRICATORS THAT HAVE
           STRENGTHS IN RELATED AREAS.

   7.4.1.5.1   <u>LIMITS OUTSIDE PEOPLE'S "LOOK"
                AT GOULD'S TOTAL MACHINE OR
                SYSTEM.</u>

7.5 ATTENTION TO DETAILS EXTREMELY IMPORTANT (SEE ARTICLES).

7.6 SIMPLICITY EXTREMELY IMPORTANT (SEE ARTICLES).

7.7 CREATIVITY IS A KEY INGREDIENT.

   7.7.1   CREATE AN ENVIRONMENT FOR CREATIVITY.

8.   CREATIVITY (SEE ARTICLES).

9.   ENGINEERS CHARACTER (SEE ARTICLES).

10.   OUTSIDE ENGINEERING OR DESIGN AND BUILD HOUSES.

   10.1 OUTSIDE SOURCES DO THINGS FOR PROFIT.

      10.1.1   IN GENERAL, THEY CANNOT SPEND THE TIME NEEDED TO
                RUN EXPERIMENTS, MAKE PROTOTYPES AND PERFECT THE
                DESIGN. EVEN IF THE FIRM IS PAID TO DO THIS,
                WHAT YOU GET IS THEIR FIRST IDEAS TRANSFORMED
                INTO DESIGNS WHICH BECOME MACHINES BROUGHT INTO
                A PLANT WHICH ARE EVENTUALLY DEBUGGED AND
                REDESIGNED TO MAKE THEM WORK.

   10.2   SPECIFICATIONS - MUST BE WRITTEN.

      10.2.1   FORCES THOUGHT AND HOMEWORK ON TASK TO BE
                ACCOMPLISHED.

      10.2.2   DRAWS FOCUS ON TASK.

         10.2.2.1   GENERATES CONSTRUCTIVE CRITICISM FROM
                     INSIDE AND OUTSIDE SOURCES.

         10.2.2.2   MINIMIZES SURPRISE.

10.2.3   SPECIFICATION MUST INSIST ON COMPLETE
          DOCUMENTATION.

          10.2.3.1   MAINTENANCE SCHEDULES CAN BE
                     ESTABLISHED.

          10.2.3.2   TROUBLESHOOTING CAN BE DONE BY
                     STUDYING ASSEMBLIES AND DETAILS.

          10.2.3.3   NEW PARTS CAN BE MADE FROM GOOD
                     DRAWINGS TO REPLACE WORN OR BROKEN
                     PARTS.

          10.2.3.4   DUPLICATE MACHINES CAN BE MADE WHEN
                     PRODUCTION DEMANDS MORE CAPACITY.

     10.2.4   IN-HOUSE WATCHDOG.

          10.2.4.1   IS NECESSARY BECAUSE OUTSIDE PERSONNEL
                     ARE NOT FAMILIAR WITH THE PROCESSES,
                     TECHNIQUES OR THE EQUIPMENT IN
                     BUILDING FUSES. THEY ARE UNAWARE OF
                     THE SUBTLE PROBLEMS THAT ARE COMMON
                     KNOWLEDGE TO THE INSIDE MECHANICAL
                     DESIGNER.

          10.2.4.2   MUST APPROVE DRAWINGS BEFORE
                     FABRICARION

          10.2.4.3   MUST BE FLEXIBLE TO RENEGOTIATE
                     PORTIONS OF JOB AS PROBLEMS ARISE.

11. OUTSIDE MACHINE SHOPS.

     11.1 MACHINE SHOPS WHO MAKE PRODUCTION MACHINES OR JIGS AND
           FIXTURES SHOULD HAVE QUALITY CONTROL.

          11.1.1 SHOPS WITH QUALITY CONTROL HAVE GOOD MACHINISTS
                  THAT CAN MAKE PARTS TO THE DRAWINGS. WHEN
                  QUALITY INSPECTORS REJECT THE PART, THE MACHINIST
                  WILL HAVE TO FIX OR REMAKE THE PART. IF A
                  MACHINIST CONTINUALLY HAS HIS PARTS REJECTED, HE
                  WILL NOT BE EMPLOYED VERY LONG AT THAT SHOP.
                  INSTEAD, HE WILL WORK FOR A MACHINE SHOP WHO
                  DOESN'T HAVE QUALITY CONTROL.

12. DESIGN MANAGEMENT (SEE ARTICLES).

13. THE FINE ART OF ENGINEERING (SEE ARTICLE).

14. QUOTES

     REAL PROGRESS IS NOT A LEAP IN THE DARK, BUT A SUCCESSION OF

MANAGEMENT

1 QUICK FIXES, PRIORITIES, CRISIS MANAGEMENT OVER COMMITTING (SEE ARTICLES).

    1.1 JUMPING FROM ONE JOB TO ANOTHER TO ANOTHER AND PUTTING OUT FIRES JUMBLES THE MIND AND GREATLY INCREASES THE TIME IT TAKES TO COMPLETE ANY JOB.

    1.2 MATCH WORK LOAD WITH CAPABILITIES OF DEPARTMENT.

    1.3 IF LARGE PORTIONS OF FACTORY PERSONNEL ARE CONSTANTLY PUTTING OUT FIRES THEN THERE ARE SERIOUS STRUCTURAL PROBLEMS.

    1.4 SPREADING PEOPLE TOO THIN BUILDS ANXIETY LEVELS, DROPS EFFECTIVENESS MEASURABLY AND EMPLOYEE TURNOVER INCREASES.

2 SHORT TERM VS LONG TERM (SEE ARTICLES)

3 DEVELOPING HUMAN RESOURCES (SEE ARTICLES)

4 VISION (SEE ARTICLES)

5 SURVIVAL (SEE ARTICLES)

6 HIGH TECH RISKS (SEE ARTICLES)

7 GENERAL COMMENTS

    7.1 WITH A STABLE , HIGHLY QUALIFIED MECHANICAL ENGINEERING DEPARTMENT WE SHOULD BE ABLE TO RESPOND TO MOST JOBS WITHIN A REASONABLE AMOUNT OF TIME, IN A PROFESSIONAL MANNER.

    7.2 WORKERS MUST HAVE TOOLS AND ENVIRONMENT THAT ALLOWS THEM TO BE SUCCESSFUL.

        7.2.1 WORK WITH THEM TO HELP THEM WIN.

        7.2.2 ALLOW THEM TO HAVE QUALITY TIME AND TO MAKE A CONCENTRATED EFFORT.

        7.2.3 LET PRIDE, NOT FEAR, BE THE DRIVING FORCE OF DOING GOOD WORK.

        7.2.4 SUCCESS BREEDS SUCCESS.

        7.2.5 LET WORKERS FEEL THE THRILL OF VICTORY AND THE AGONY OF DEFEAT.

    7.3 QUALITY CAN BE THE DRIVING FORCE IN DEVELOPING TECHNOLOGIES, MACHINES, ETC.

    7.4 CONCENTRATED EFFORT MUST BE PREVALENT ON THE MAJOR PROJECTS WITH A PROGRAM MANAGER ASSIGNED TO IT AND GIVEN RESPONSIBILITY FOR IT.

7.5 ALL MACHINE DESIGN SHOULD BE DONE THROUGH MANUFACTURING ENGINEERING.
     ALL JIGS, FIXTURES AND MACHINE DESIGN DRAWINGS SHOULD BE KEPT IN
     MANUFACTURING ENGINEERING DEPARTMENT ALONG WITH OPERATING MANUALS.

7.6 ENGINEERING GROUND WORK, INVESTIGATION AND PRELIMINARAY
     CALCULATIONS SHOW NO IMMEDIATE RESULTS;
     HOWEVER, IN TIME, THE PAY OFF IS SUBSTANTIAL AND CAN INFLUENCE
     A COMPANY'S CHANCE FOR SURVIVAL.

7.7 COMPANY IS LIKE A MACHINE; ALL PARTS MUST FUNCTION PROPERLY FOR
     IT TO RUN WELL. WHEN ALL PARTS FUNCTION WELL, PROFITS CAN SOAR.
     IF ONE PART FAILS, THE MACHINE'S FUNCTION IS IN JEOPARDY, BUT
     EASY TO TROUBLESHOOT. IF MORE THAN ONE PART IS NOT RUNNING
     PROPERLY, IT BECOMES DIFFICULT TO PINPOINT PROBLEMS.

7.8 DECISIONS MUST BE MADE AT LOWEST POSSIBLE LEVEL.

7.9 SEPARATE LONG TERM JOBS FROM SHORT TERM JOBS AS MUCH AS POSSIBLE.

C O M M O N   T H R E A D S
////////////////////////////

FLEXIBILITY: FAMILIES

                        - BRAIDER   .20 THRU 3.0 OD

                        - DRILL & PIN MACH   1.0 THRU 3.0 OD

                        - ROTARY FILL MACH   1.0 THRU 3.0 OD

                        - CRIMPING MACH (SMALL) .37 THRU 1.0 OD

                        - CRIMPING MACH (LARGE) 1.0 THRU 3.0 OD

                        - BELT WINDER   .18 THRU 1.0 ID

                        - STEIMER TUBE WINDER   .18 THRU 3.5+ ID

                        - BUILDING FIXT   ALL CABLE PROTEC

DOCUMENTATION: - FOR EVOLVING DESIGNS

                        - FOR REPEATING DESIGNS

                        - FOR STANDARDIZING DESIGNS

QUICK CHANGEOVER

STANDARDIZE METHODS

CONTROL ALL PARAMETERS

MODULAR CONSTRUCTION

EVOLUTION OF DESIGNS

MAXIMUM USE OF COMMERCIAL PARTS

COST vs TOLERANCE

The use of appropriate tolerance is naturally an important responsibility of product designers considering production capabilities, part function and ease of assembly. Tolerances that are closer than necessary contribute nothing to the design except to inflate costs. See Figure 3.

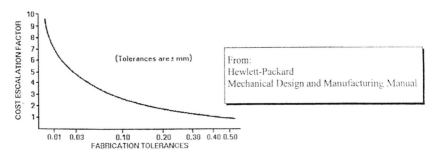

(Tolerances are ± mm)

From:
Hewlett-Packard
Mechanical Design and Manufacturing Manual

Fabrication Tolerances (± mm)
Figure 3. Cost vs. Tolerance

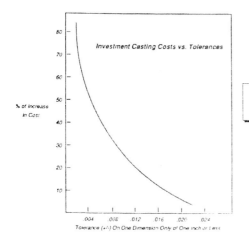

From:
The Competitive Product Development Institute

Author – Career Notes

Don Hadfield's first job out of college was with Norton Company's Machine Tool Division, where he learned the process of classical engineering. He then moved on to Texas Instruments, working in a high-powered group designing automated equipment and went on to Simplex Wire & Cable Company and became its Chief Mechanical Engineer working under Norm McNerney. After, over twelve years, he went to Gould, where he was Supervisor of Machine Design. At Gould, he taught a number of Northeastern University co-op students the art and science of machine design. At Simplex and Gould, he was close enough to their presidents to understand their entrepreneurial spirit and vision. His last job took him to Hewlett- Packard, which he considered, at that time, to be one of the best companies in the world to work for. At Hewlett-Packard, Kate Stohlman, a master at building a team, put together the most powerful one he had ever seen. She hired Jon Rourke, who, in turn, hired Don. Jon was a true entrepreneur. He was one of the very few that Don worked with who understood the whole process: the business side, machine design, product design, fabrication processes and the manufacturing processes. That team and the "HP Way" had major impact on many of the leading-edge products and critical, complex processes that are used today. Along the way, Mr. Hadfield was offered a number of much higher positions, one being VP of Engineering, which was offered by the president and VP of Tyco, who knew of Mr. Hadfield's engineering capabilities. He declined the offer, because it would have taken him away from what he loved to do most—mechanical engineering—and felt it would compromise his family.

Mr. Hadfield had a passion for design and wanted it perfect. As he matured, he realized that perfect was too nebulous. Instead, he strived for perfection but settled for excellence,

Author – Career Notes

learning from every design. Most of his designs were used in the plant where he worked. Feedback was always welcome, including from those who built his designs as well as those who used them. If he was to do it over, what ideas would be used again or which ones could be improved upon? How could it have been done better? He felt one had to be humble to receive the feedback, negative as well as positive. Mr. Hadfield, in his 45-year career, designed a wide variety of equipment: automatic assembly equipment, semi-automatic machines, assembly tooling, high-pressure terminations, machining devices for pipe used on offshore oil and gas platforms, and a wide variety of continuous processing equipment. He has several patents related to these projects. He had to deal with a number of Engineering and Operations VPs, motivating him to develop a guide called "Machine Design and Related Subjects" (see Appendix). Imbedded in this manual is what Mr. Hadfield called "The Basic Truths of In-Plant Machine Design." It was in outline form, and each item or point was verified by articles from trade magazines, trade journals, and academic studies. This was used to teach and show how engineering is done, revealing the mantra of his machine design group. He was not about to be compromised by people who didn't understand the process.

Mr. Hadfield became a student of design, and over the years, as the nuggets revealed themselves, he recorded them, all of which are in this book. Even though it is based on proven ways and common sense, he feels it needs to be stated in clear language, used as a guide for young engineers and for reinforcement of the right way.

Made in the USA
Middletown, DE
07 September 2017